FAITH

90 DEVOTIONS FROM

OUR DAILY BREAD

COMPILED BY DAVE BRANON

Discovery House.
from Our Daily Bread Ministries

Discovery House is affiliated with Our Daily Bread Ministries,
Grand Rapids, Michigan.

Requests for permission to quote from this book should be directed to:
Permissions Department, Discovery House, P.O. Box 3566, Grand
Rapids, MI 49501, or contact us by e-mail at permissionsdept@dhp.org.

ISBN: 978-1-62707-659-3

Printed in the United States of America

First printing in 2016

CONTENTS

FOREWORD

Fans of a sports team are often referred to as "the faithful."

A play-by-play announcer may look out over the crowd at a ball game and say, "There is great anticipation tonight among the faithful as the team's ace takes the field."

Those who support and cheer for and often live-and-die with the fortunes of their team are called "faithful" because of their unwavering devotion. The truly faithful go to games whether the team is in first place or in last.

It's a nice word: *faithful*. It suggests belief in something. In loyalty. In the determination to never abandon what one loves.

And it suggests being full of faith.

In the Old Testament book of Psalms, the writers show how God cares for people of faith—people who are faithful to God.

Those who are faithful are promised God's *presence*. Psalm 37:28 says, "The Lord loves the just and will not forsake his faithful ones." Those who are faithful to God can depend on His continual presence in their lives—His promise not to forsake them.

Also, the faithful are promised *peace*. The writer explains: "[The Lord] promises peace to his people, his faithful servants" (85:8). There is an inexplicable, unfathomable peace that calms the hearts of those who have put their faith in God (see Philippians 4:7).

God offers His *protection* to those who believe in Him with a heart of faith. "He guards the lives of his faithful ones and delivers them from the hand of the wicked," He says in Psalm 97:10. We relax in our faith, comforted in the constant watchful gaze of the omniscient one.

Then comes the ultimate reward. When God in His sovereignty takes us from this world to dwell in heaven's glories, the faithful are viewed as *precious*. "Precious in the sight of the LORD is the death of his faithful servants" (Psalm 116:15).

If all this is ours because of faith, it would seem logical that we would want to know all we can about faith and how it works in our lives. If God honors us for our faith, how helpful would it be to dive in to the subject and see it as clearly as possible?

That is where this book comes in. In *Faith: 90 Devotions from Our Daily Bread*, we have selected dozens of articles that remind us about faith, challenge us in our faith walk, and encourage us to elevate faith to its right spot as the essence of our relationship with our Lord and Savior.

It is our prayer that the variety of authors and articles in this book will give you a wide-ranging approach and a well-rounded appreciation for what it means to be faithful. We hope you can spend some time with these articles and find your faith in God rising to new vistas of enjoyment.

Our desire for you as you read this book is similar to Paul's in the book of Philippians when he told "the faithful" of his day that he wanted for them "progress and joy in the faith" (1:25).

—*Dave Branon*
Our Daily Bread writer

THE FAMILY OF FAITH

Read: 1 Thessalonians 2:6-14

Because we loved you so much, we were delighted to share with you not only the gospel of God but our lives as well. —1 THESSALONIANS 2:8

During the 1980s, a singles' class at our church became a close-knit family for many people who had lost a spouse through divorce or death. When someone needed to move, class members packed boxes, carried furniture, and provided food. Birthdays and holidays were no longer solitary events as faith and friendship merged into an ongoing relationship of encouragement. Many of those bonds forged during adversity all those years ago continue to flourish and sustain individuals and families today.

Paul's letter to the followers of Jesus in Thessalonica paints a picture of life-giving relationships in God's family. "We were gentle among you, just as a nursing mother cherishes her own children" (1 Thessalonians 2:7 NKJV). "For you remember, [brothers and sisters], our labor and toil . . . that we might not be a burden to any of you" (v. 9). "We exhorted, and comforted, and charged every one of you, as a father does his own children" (v. 11). Like mothers, fathers, brothers, and sisters, Paul and his associates shared the gospel and their lives with these fellow believers who "had become dear" to them (v. 8).

In God's family of faith, He provides mothers, fathers, sisters, and brothers for us. The Lord gives His joy as we share our lives together in His grace and love.

—*David McCasland*

The ultimate ground of faith and knowledge is confidence in God. —Charles Hodge

ROOTED

Read: 2 Chronicles 24:15-22

Joash did what was right in the eyes of the Lord all the years of Jehoiada the priest. —2 CHRONICLES 24:2

Joash must have been confused and frightened when he was told about the evil deeds of his grandmother Athaliah. She had murdered his brothers to usurp the power of the throne in Judah. But baby Joash had been safely hidden away by his his aunt and uncle for six years (2 Chronicles 22:10–12). As he grew, he enjoyed the love and instruction of his caregivers. When Joash was only seven years old, he was secretly crowned king and his grandmother was overthrown (23:12–15).

Young King Joash had a wise counselor by his side—his very own Uncle Jehoiada (chapters 22–25). Joash was one of the rare "good kings" of Judah, and while his uncle was alive he obeyed the Lord by doing right (24:2). But once his uncle was no longer there to teach and lead by example, Joash fell away and his life ended badly (24:15–25). It seems that the roots of his faith did not run very deep. He even began to worship idols. Perhaps Joash's "faith" had been more his uncle's than his own.

Others can teach us the principles of their faith, but each of us must come individually to a lasting and personal faith in Christ. For faith to be real, it must become our own. God will help us walk with Him and become rooted and established in the faith (Colossians 2:6–7).

—*Cindy Hess Kasper*

The faith that continues to the end gives proof that it was genuine in the beginning.

NO RISK

Read: Ephesians 2:1–10

For it is by grace you have been saved, through faith—and this is not from yourselves, it is the gift of God. —EPHESIANS 2:8

A colleague recently shared an experience I don't intend to try personally—bungee jumping. I found his description of the event both fascinating and terrifying. To think of jumping headfirst from a bridge hundreds of feet in the air suspended only by a giant rubber band is not my idea of a good time. But his leap was not without support. He described not one, but two heavy-duty harnesses that secured him to his lifeline—and to safety. The careful design and proven testing of those harnesses gave him great confidence as he jumped into the air.

As I listened, it occurred to me that for the follower of Christ, living in a sinful world is not a blind "leap of faith." We too have a pair of protections that can secure us in even the darkest times of life. In Ephesians 2:8–9, Paul wrote these words, "For it is by grace you have been saved, through faith—and this is not from yourselves, it is the gift of God—not by works, so that no one can boast."

It's in these twin harnesses—God's grace and faith in the finished work of Jesus—that our relationship with God safely rests. In the strength of these provisions, salvation is not a risky leap into the void. It's an exercise of confidence in God's Word and His unfailing love and protection.

—*Bill Crowder*

We can expect God's peace when we accept God's grace.

THE LEGACY

Read: Colossians 3:8-17

Therefore, as God's chosen people, holy and dearly loved, clothe yourselves with compassion, kindness, humility, gentleness and patience.
—COLOSSIANS 3:12

One day my wife called me at work and said, "Something's going on next door. Lots of cars are there." Because of my neighbor's occupation, I feared the worst, and soon those fears were realized. Our neighbor, policeman Trevor Slot, had just been killed in the line of duty, trying to stop the escape of two bank robbers. Our community was stunned.

Trevor had no time to prepare for his death. Yet he was ready. His faith in Christ was secure, and his reputation as a remarkable man was intact. At his funeral, attended by hundreds of fellow officers, his colleague Detective Brandyn Heugel said, "He was a dedicated police officer, but first and foremost he was a loving husband to Kim and a doting father to Kaitlyn and Abbie." Indeed the theme of Trevor's tributes all centered on his great personality and his love and care for his family.

Trevor's life exemplified the words of Colossians 3:12–13, "Clothe yourselves with compassion, kindness, humility, gentleness and patience. Bear with each other and forgive one another." Those traits leave an inspiring legacy.

We don't know when God will call us home, but we do know this: Each day is an opportunity to leave a testimony worthy of our faith.

—*Dave Branon*

Each day we add to our legacy—
good or bad.

☒

THE DEFEAT OF DEATH

Read: 1 Thessalonians 4:15-18

*But thanks be to God! He gives us the victory through our Lord
Jesus Christ.* —1 CORINTHIANS 15:57

One of the greatest tests of our trust in the gospel of Jesus
Christ is how we react in the face of death. When we attend
a memorial service for a departed friend who loved the Lord
Jesus, we gather to honor a believer whose stalwart trust has
richly blessed the lives of those who knew him. The words spo-
ken are more an expression of praise to God than a tribute
to an admired fellow pilgrim. The service is a God-glorifying
testimony to our Savior's victory over death and the grave
(1 Corinthians 15:54–57).

How different from the empty funeral service of Charles
Bradlaugh, a belligerent British atheist. Writer Arthur Porritt
recalls: "No prayer was said at the grave. Indeed, not a single
word was uttered. The remains, placed in a light coffin, were
lowered into the earth in a quite unceremonious fashion as
if carrion were being hustled out of sight. . . . I came away
heart-frozen. It only then dawned on me that loss of faith in
the continuity of human personality after death gives death an
appalling victory."

Christians, however, believe in a face-to-face fellowship
with our Lord after death and the eventual resurrection of our
bodies (1 Corinthians 15:42–55; 1 Thessalonians 4:15–18).
Does your faith rejoice in victory over death?

—*Vernon Grounds*

Because Christ is alive, we too shall live.

DANGEROUS FREEDOM

Read: Galatians 5:1-6; 16-21

You, my brothers and sisters, were called to be free. But do not use your freedom to indulge the flesh; rather, serve one another humbly in love.
—GALATIANS 5:13

Freedom is dangerous in the hands of those who don't know how to use it. That's why criminals are confined in prisons with barbed wire, steel bars, and concrete barriers. Or consider a campfire that is allowed to spread in a dry forest. It quickly becomes a blazing inferno. Unchecked freedom can create chaos.

Nowhere is this more evident than in the Christian life. Believers are free from the law's curse, its penalty, and its guilt-producing power. Fear, anxiety, and guilt are replaced by peace, forgiveness, and liberty. Who could be more free than one who is free in the depths of his soul? But here is where we could fail. It is possible to use freedom's luxury to live selfishly or to claim ownership of what God has merely entrusted to us.

The proper use of freedom is "faith working through love" to serve one another (Galatians 5:6, 13). When we rely on the Spirit and use our energies to love God and help others, we can always use our liberty to build up, not to tear down.

Freedom without limits can be dangerous. Instead, let's "serve one another humbly in love."

—*Dennis DeHaan*

Freedom doesn't give us the right to do what we please, but to do what pleases God.

BAD FAITH, GOOD FAITH

Read: Romans 4:18-25

He did not waver through unbelief regarding the promise of God, but was strengthened in his faith and gave glory to God. —ROMANS 4:20

"You gotta have faith," people say. But what does that mean? Is *any* and every faith good faith?

"Believe in yourself and all that you are," wrote one positive thinker a century ago. "Know that there is something inside you that is greater than any obstacle." As nice as that may sound, it falls to pieces when it crashes into reality. We need a faith in something bigger than ourselves.

God promised Abram he would have a multitude of descendants (Genesis 15:4–5), but he faced a huge obstacle—he was old and childless. When he and Sarai got tired of waiting for God to make good on His promise, they tried to overcome that obstacle on their own. As a result, they fractured their family and created a lot of unnecessary dissension (see Genesis 16 and 21:8–21).

Nothing Abraham did in his own strength worked. But ultimately he became known as a man of tremendous faith. Paul wrote of him, "Against all hope, Abraham in hope believed and so became the father of many nations, just as it had been said to him, 'So shall your offspring be'" (Romans 4:18). This faith, said Paul, "was credited to him as righteousness" (v. 22).

Abraham's faith was in something far bigger than himself—the one and only God. It's the object of our faith that makes all the difference.

—*Tim Gustafson*

———

Our faith is good if it's in the right Person.

ALL WE NEED TO KNOW

Read: Romans 7:18-25

For I know that good itself does not dwell in me, that is, in my sinful nature. For I have the desire to do what is good, but I cannot carry it out.
—ROMANS 7:18

In a Fernando Ortega rendition of "Just As I Am," Billy Graham's voice can be heard faintly in the background. Dr. Graham is reminiscing about an illness during which he believed he was dying. As he mused on his past, he realized what a great sinner he was and how much he continues to need God's daily forgiveness.

Billy Graham was putting an end to the notion that apart from God we're okay. We can feel good about ourselves, but that confidence must come from the knowledge that we're greatly loved children of God (John 3:16), not that we're very good children (Romans 7:18).

The first step in becoming a truly "good" person as a follower of Christ is to stop pretending that we're good on our own and to ask God to make us as good as we can be. We will fail many times, but He will keep growing us and changing us. God is faithful and—in His time and in His way—He'll do it.

In his final years, the writer of "Amazing Grace," John Newton, suffered from dementia and lamented the loss of his memory. Yet he confided, "I do remember two things: I am a great sinner, and Jesus is a great Savior." When it comes to faith, those are the only things anyone needs to know.

—*David Roper*

God's grace accepted is God's peace experienced.

T-BALL FAITH

Read: Luke 15:1-7

Nehemiah said, "Go and enjoy choice food and sweet drinks, and send some to those who have nothing prepared. This day is holy to our Lord. Do not grieve, for the joy of the LORD is your strength." —NEHEMIAH 8:10

Whoever dreamed up T-ball is a genius: Every kid on the field gets a taste of the fun and joy of the game before they taste the disappointment of striking out.

In T-ball, a baseball is placed on a rubber tee about waist-high to the five- and six-year-old batters. Players swing until they hit the ball, and then they run. On my first night as a coach, the very first batter hit the ball far into the outfield. Suddenly every player from every position ran to get the ball instead of staying where they were supposed to. When one of them reached it, there was nobody left in the infield for him to throw it to! All the players were standing together—cheering with unrestrained exuberance!

Those who have recently come to know Jesus as Savior have an unrestrained joy that is a delight to be around as well. We rejoice with them, and so do the angels in heaven! (Luke 15:7). New Christians are in love with God and excited about knowing Him and learning from His Word.

Those who've been Christians for a long time may get discouraged with the struggles of the Christian life and forget the joy of newfound faith. So take the opportunity to rejoice with those who've recently come to faith. God can use them to inspire you to renew your own commitment to Jesus.

—*Randy Kilgore*

Restore to me the joy of your salvation.

Psalm 51:12

⟨⟩

ANCHORS IN THE STORM

Read: Joshua 1:1-9

"Have I not commanded you? Be strong and courageous.
Do not be afraid; do not be discouraged, for the LORD your God
will be with you wherever you go." —JOSHUA 1:9

When Matt and Jessica tried to navigate their sailboat into a Florida inlet during Hurricane Sandy, the craft ran aground. As the waves crashed around them, they quickly dropped anchor. It held the sailboat in place until they could be rescued. They said that if they had not put down the anchor, "We would have lost our boat for sure." Without the anchor, the relentless waves would have smashed the vessel onto the shore.

We need anchors that hold us secure in our spiritual lives as well. When God called Joshua to lead His people after Moses's death, He gave him anchors of promise he could rely on in troubled times. The Lord said to him, "I will be with you. I will never leave you nor forsake you. . . . The LORD your God will be with you wherever you go" (Joshua 1:5, 9). God also gave Joshua and His people the "Book of the Law" to study and observe (vv. 7–8). That, and God's presence, were anchors the Israelites could rely on as they faced many challenges.

When we're in the middle of suffering or when doubts start threatening our faith, what are our anchors? We could start with Joshua 1:5. Although our faith may feel weak, if it's anchored in God's promises and presence, He will safely hold us.

—*Anne Cetas*

When we feel the stress of the storm we learn the strength of the anchor.

FAITH WITH WORKS

Read: James 2:14-26

Faith by itself, if it is not accompanied by action, is dead.
—JAMES 2:17

Because of his arthritis, Roger could no longer handle the winters of Illinois, so he moved to tropical Bangkok, Thailand. One day he remembered his grandmother's favorite song, "What You Are." The lyrics from this song of long ago say: "What you are speaks so loud that the world can't hear what you say; they're looking at your walk, not listening to your talk; they're judging from your actions every day."

This song prompted Roger to feed the homeless who stayed along a half-mile stretch of road. Every morning, he served hot food to more than forty-five families. Years later, one of the homeless women came to know Jesus as Savior and sought out Roger to thank him for introducing her to the love of Christ.

In James, we are clearly told that faith without action is dead (2:17). It does not mean that works will result in faith, but that our good works will affirm that our faith is real. It is easy to say we believe in God, but only our works can prove the truthfulness of our words. Abraham was an example of this. He didn't just talk about his faith; he demonstrated it by his willingness to give up his only son in obedience to God (James 2:21–24; see Genesis 22:1–18). And Isaac was spared.

Today, how can we actively demonstrate our love for God and trust in Him?

—*Albert Lee*

———

What matters is not faith and works; it is not faith or works; it is faith that works.

FOOD IN THE CUPBOARD

Read: Matthew 6:25-34

"Therefore I tell you, do not worry about your life, what you will eat or drink; or about your body, what you will wear. Is not life more than food, and the body more than clothes?" —MATTHEW 6:25

My friend Marcia, the director of the Jamaica Christian School for the Deaf, recently illustrated an important way to look at things. In a newsletter article she titled "A Blessed Start," she pointed out that for the first time in seven years the school began the new year with a surplus. And what was that surplus? A thousand dollars in the bank? No. Enough school supplies for the year? No. It was simply this: A month's supply of food in the cupboard.

When you're in charge of feeding thirty hungry boarding students on a shoestring budget, that's big! She accompanied her note with this verse from 1 Chronicles 16:34: "Oh, give thanks to the LORD, for He is good! For His mercy endures forever" (NKJV).

Year after year Marcia trusts God to provide for the children and staff at her school. She never has much—whether it's water or food or school supplies. Yet she is always grateful for what God sends, and she is faithful to believe that He will continue to provide.

As we begin a new year, do we have faith in God's provision? To do so is to take our Savior at His word when He said, "Do not worry about your life, . . . Do not worry about tomorrow" (Matthew 6:25, 34).

—*Dave Branon*

Worry does not empty tomorrow of its sorrow; it empties today of its strength. —Corrie ten Boom

CHILDLIKE FAITH

Read Matthew 8:5–10

Jesus replied, "What is impossible with man is possible with God."
—LUKE 18:27

On the way home from a family camping trip, six-year-old Tanya and her dad were the only ones still awake in the car. As Tanya looked at the full moon through the car window, she asked, "Daddy, do you think I can touch the moon if I stand on my tiptoes?"

"No, I don't think so," he smiled.

"Can you reach it?"

"No, I don't think I can either."

She was quiet for a moment, then she said confidently, "Daddy, maybe if you hold me up on your shoulders?"

Faith? Yes—the childlike faith that daddies can do anything. True faith, though, has the written promise of God for its foundation. In Hebrews 11:1, we read, "Faith is confidence in what we hope for and assurance about what we do not see." Jesus talked a lot about faith, and throughout the Gospels we read of His response to those who had great faith.

When a paralyzed man's friends brought him to Jesus, He "saw their faith," forgave the man of his sins, and healed him (Matthew 9:2–6). When the centurion asked Jesus to "say the word, and my servant will be healed" (8:8), Jesus "was amazed" and said, "I have not found anyone in Israel with such great faith" (8:10).

When we have faith in God, we will find that all things are possible (Luke 18:27).

—*Cindy Hess Kasper*

———

A childlike faith unlocks the door to the kingdom of heaven.

FAITH AND RICHES

Read Ephesians 1

I pray that the eyes of your heart may be enlightened in order that you may know the hope to which he has called you, the riches of his glorious inheritance in his holy people. —EPHESIANS 1:18

Do you want to be rich? Do you think your faith will bring you riches? What kind of riches are you looking for?

There's good news and bad news if wealth is what you want. The good news is that God's Word does promise riches to the believer. The "bad" news is that it doesn't have anything to do with money.

Here are some examples of the riches that can be ours as believers in Jesus Christ:

- An understanding of God the Father and the Son, "in whom are hidden all the treasures of wisdom and knowledge" (Colossians 2:2–3).
- Christ, "the hope of glory," living in us (Colossians 1:27).
- Mighty strength in our inner being, "through his Spirit" (Ephesians 3:16).
- Having all our needs met by God (Philippians 4:19).
- The "wisdom and knowledge of God" (Romans 11:33).
- "Redemption through his blood, the forgiveness of sins," which comes from God's grace (Ephesians 1:7).

Yes, God's Word promises us great riches—treasures that we cannot even attempt to purchase with any amount of money. It is these riches that we must seek, enjoy, and use to glorify their source—our heavenly Father.

—*Dave Branon*

God's Word promises riches
that money cannot buy.

Ж

STILL IN GOD'S HANDS

Read: Job 1:13-22

In all this, Job did not sin by charging God with wrongdoing.
—JOB 1:22

During my first year of seminary, I listened as a new friend described her life. Abandoned by her husband, she was raising two small children alone. Earning just over minimum wage, she had little chance of escaping the poverty and dangers she described in her neighborhood.

As a father, I was moved by her concern for her children and asked, "How do you handle all of this?" She seemed surprised by my question and replied, "We are doing all we can do, and I must leave them in God's hands." Her trust in God in the midst of trials reminded me of Job's trust (1:6–22).

A year later, she phoned and asked if I would come be with her at the funeral home. Her son had been killed in a drive-by shooting. I asked God for words to comfort her and for the wisdom not to try to explain the unexplainable.

Standing with her that day, however, I marveled as again and again she comforted others—her confidence in God unshaken by this terrible blow. Turning to me as we parted, her final words were a poignant reminder of the depth of her faith: "My boy is still in God's hands." Like Job, she "did not sin by charging God with wrongdoing"(v. 22).

We too can develop an unshakable faith as we daily live in fellowship with the Lord.

—*Randy Kilgore*

Nothing can shake those who are secure in God's hands.

FAITH MIXED WITH DOUBT

Read: Psalm 42

Why, my soul, are you downcast? Why so disturbed within me?
Put your hope in God, for I will yet praise him, my Savior and my God.
—PSALM 42:11

When my close friend Sharon was killed in a car accident, my heart broke. I'm ashamed to admit it, but when life's circumstances hurt so much, my faith is often mixed with doubt. When Sharon died, I cried out to God with these questions:

Lord, I sure don't understand you. Why did you allow this death? "Have you not heard? The everlasting God . . . neither faints nor is weary. His understanding is unsearchable" (Isaiah 40:28 NKJV). " 'My thoughts are not your thoughts, neither are your ways my ways,' declares the LORD" (Isaiah 55:8).

Lord, you are beyond my understanding. But I still wonder: Have you turned your back on the world? "God is seated on his holy throne" (Psalm 47:8) and "rules forever by his power" (66:7).

Lord, I do believe you are ruling this world, but do you care about the pain? Have you forgotten to be good? I am "good and ready to forgive, and abundant in mercy to all those who call upon [Me]" (Psalm 86:5 NKJV).

Yes, Lord, you have been good to me in countless ways, including listening to my doubts and questions about you.

The answers God gives us in His Word may not take away our sadness, but we can always rest in the truth that He is wise, sovereign, and good.

—*Anne Cetas*

Every loss leaves an empty space that only God's presence can fill.

GOD'S GOOD HEART

Read: Romans 5:1-11

Consider it pure joy, my brothers and sisters, whenever you face trials of many kinds. —JAMES 1:2

Roger had been through a lot. He had open-heart surgery to repair a leaky valve. Then, within just a couple of weeks, doctors had to perform the surgery again because of complications. He had just begun to heal with physical therapy when he had a biking accident and broke his collarbone. Added to this, Roger also experienced the heartbreak of losing his mother during this time. He became very discouraged. When a friend asked him if he had seen God at work in any small ways, he confessed that he really didn't feel he had.

I appreciate Roger's honesty. Feelings of discouragement or doubt are part of my life too. In Romans, the apostle Paul says, "We can rejoice . . . when we run into problems and trials, for we know that they help us develop endurance. And endurance develops strength of character, and character strengthens our confident hope of salvation" (5:3–4 NLT). But that doesn't mean we always feel the joy. We may just need someone to sit down and listen to us pour out our hearts, and to talk with God. Sometimes it takes looking back on the situation before we see how our faith has grown during trials and doubts.

Knowing that God wants to use our difficulties to strengthen our faith can help us to trust His good heart for us.

—*Anne Cetas*

God may lead us into troubled waters to deepen our trust in Him.

THE OBJECT OF OUR FAITH

Read: Matthew 17:14–21

He replied, "Because you have so little faith. Truly I tell you, if you have faith as small as a mustard seed, you can say to this mountain, 'Move from here to there,' and it will move. Nothing will be impossible for you."
—MATTHEW 17:20

Suppose someone asks you to take a ride in his single-engine plane. You politely decline. Why? Well, you've heard that the plane has a history of mechanical problems, and you don't have confidence in its safety. The pilot assures you that he fearlessly entrusts his life to it whenever he flies. You still decline. A few weeks later the plane crashes, and he is killed. An investigation shows that the engine was faulty. The pilot had strong faith—but it was faith in a faulty object.

Many of us who are sincere Christians worry that our faith seems too small. But we need to distinguish between the size of our faith and the object of our faith.

Jesus taught that if we have faith no bigger than a tiny seed (Matthew 17:20), God will respond to our prayers according to His will, wisdom, and grace (1 John 5:14–15). He hears the faintest cry of our hearts, the feeblest whisper of our lips, and in love He listens and responds to our faith (Matthew 14:26–31).

No matter how small and insufficient we think our faith is, let's keep on praying. Remember, it is the object of our faith—our Almighty God—not the size of our faith that is all-important.

—*Vernon Grounds*

Faith must focus on God, not on itself.

VISIBLE VULNERABILITY

Read: Ephesians 4:2-6

*Be completely humble and gentle; be patient, bearing with
one another in love.* —EPHESIANS 4:2

As I ventured out several weeks after shoulder surgery, I was fearful. I had become comfortable using my arm sling, but both my surgeon and physical therapist now told me to stop wearing it. That's when I saw this statement: "At this stage, sling wear is discouraged except as a *visible sign of vulnerability* in an uncontrolled environment."

Ah, that was it! I feared the enthusiastic person who might give me a bear hug or the unaware friend who might bump me accidentally. I was hiding behind my flimsy baby-blue sling because I feared being hurt.

Allowing ourselves to be vulnerable can be scary. We want to be loved and accepted for who we are, but we fear that if people truly knew us, they would reject us and we could get hurt. What if they found out we are not smart enough . . . kind enough . . . good enough?

But as members of God's family, we have a responsibility to help each other grow in faith. We're told to "encourage one another," to "build each other up" (1 Thessalonians 5:11), and to "be patient, bearing with one another in love" (Ephesians 4:2).

When we are honest and vulnerable with other believers, we may discover we have mutual struggles battling temptation or learning how to live obediently. But most of all, we will share the wonder of God's gift of grace in our lives.

—*Cindy Hess Kasper*

Being honest about our struggles allows us to help each other.

EYES OF FAITH

Read: John 4:46-54

For we live by faith, not by sight. —2 CORINTHIANS 5:7

God sometimes answers our prayers in marvelous ways, but He does not want us to become preoccupied with the miraculous. That's why Jesus gently rebuked the nobleman who begged Him to come and heal his son (John 4:48). But in response to the father's repeated appeal He said, "Go, your son will live" (v. 50). The father came to "believe" on the basis of Jesus's word alone. The reality of his faith is seen in the fact that he obeyed Christ's simple command and "departed."

Upon returning home, the nobleman discovered that his son had been healed "at one in the afternoon" on the previous day. From his servants he learned exactly what had taken place and when. His son was made well at the same instant that Jesus said, "Your son will live" (vv. 50–53).

At times we are amazed by God's perfect timing and miraculous intervention when He answers our prayers. We must be careful, though, not to become so preoccupied with the miracle that we forget the One who performed it. We need to remain focused on Christ, whether a miracle takes place or not.

Sooner or later we will be called upon to trust God as we endure sickness, grief, or disappointment. That's when "we live by faith, not by sight" (2 Corinthians 5:7).

—*Herb Vander Lugt*

Believing is seeing what our eyes cannot see.

IN EVERY GENERATION

Read: Psalm 100

For the LORD is good and his love endures forever;
his faithfulness continues through all generations. —PSALM 100:5

It may seem surprising when children don't follow their parents' example of faith in God. Equally unexpected is a person with a deep commitment to Christ who emerges from a family where faith was not present. In every generation, each person has a choice.

Samuel was a great man of God who appointed his two sons, Joel and Abijah, as leaders over Israel (1 Samuel 8:1–2). Unlike their father, however, they were corrupt and "turned aside after dishonest gain and accepted bribes and perverted justice" (v. 3). Yet, years later, we find Heman, Joel's son, appointed as a musician in the house of the Lord (1 Chronicles 6:31–33). Heman, Samuel's grandson—along with Asaph, his right-hand man and the author of many of the psalms—served the Lord by singing joyful songs (1 Chronicles 15:16–17).

Even though a person seems indifferent toward the faith so precious to his or her parents, God is still at work. Things can change in later years, and seeds of faith may spring to life in generations to come.

No matter what the family situation may be, we know that "the LORD is good and his love endures forever; his faithfulness continues through all generations."

—*David McCasland*

God's faithfulness extends to all generations.

UNFALTERING FAITH

Read: Job 2:1-10

"Naked I came from my mother's womb, and naked I will depart.
The LORD gave and the LORD has taken away; may the name
of the LORD be praised." —JOB 1:21

Scottish author Sir Walter Scott faced financial disaster when his publisher went bankrupt in 1826. He was heavily invested in the firm, and it appeared that he would lose everything, including Abbotsford, his castlelike home. A Christian of unwavering faith, he wrote in his journal, "Things are so much worse than I apprehended that I shall neither save Abbotsford nor anything else. Naked we entered the world and naked we leave it. Blessed be the name of the Lord."

A life that doesn't undergo heartbreaking adversity is rare. Job was not overstating our common experience when he lamented, "Mortals, born of woman, are of few days and full of trouble" (Job 14:1).

Many of us talk about loss and suffering and argue about why evil things happen to good people. But it's quite different to deal victoriously with the painful experiences that happen to us personally. What we really need in the teeth of affliction is not a plausible explanation but the ability to endure without emotional collapse or spiritual bitterness. We need the sustaining confidence that enables us to believe in God's love and wisdom (1:21; 2:10).

Pray for an unfaltering faith that stands strong under life's greatest pressures.

—Vernon Grounds

Great faith is often built during great trials.

THE SMALL GIANT

1 Samuel 17:32-37

David said to Saul, . . . "The Lord who rescued me from the paw of the lion and the paw of the bear will rescue me from the hand of this Philistine." Saul said to David, "Go, and the LORD be with you."
—1 SAMUEL 17:37

The towering enemy strides into the Valley of Elah. He stands nine feet tall, and his coat of armor, made of many small bronze plates, glimmers in the sunlight. The shaft of his spear is wrapped with cords so it can spin through the air and be thrown with greater distance and accuracy. Goliath looks invincible.

But David knows better. While Goliath may look like a giant and act like a giant, in contrast to the living God he is small. David has a right view of God and therefore a right view of the circumstances. He sees Goliath as one who is defying the armies of the living God (1 Samuel 17:26). He confidently appears before Goliath in his shepherd's clothes, armed with only his staff, five stones, and a sling. His confidence is not in what he has but in who is with him (v. 45).

What "Goliath" are you facing right now? It may be an impossible situation at work, a financial difficulty, or a broken relationship. With God all things are small in comparison. Nothing is too big for Him. The words of the hymnwriter Charles Wesley remind us: "Faith, mighty faith, the promise sees, and looks to that alone; laughs at impossibilities, and cries 'it shall be done!'" God is able to deliver you if that's His desire, and He may do so in ways you don't expect.

—*Poh Fang Chia*

———

Don't tell God how big your giants are. Tell your giants how big your God is.

AN INSTRUCTED FAITH

Read: Ecclesiastes 3:16–4:3

For what I received I passed on to you as of first importance:
that Christ died for our sins according to the Scriptures, that he was
buried, that he was raised on the third day according to the Scriptures.
—1 CORINTHIANS 15:3–4

When I witness to people about Christ, I often hear this response: "I'm all right, I have a strong faith." But our discussions soon reveal that all they have is faith in faith. Genuine saving faith, though, is based on the truth of God's Word.

Billy Graham made this clear during an interview on a TV talk show. He said he eagerly anticipates death because he expects to be with Jesus. He went on to explain that his confidence rests on what the Bible says about Christ's sacrificial death and resurrection. The interviewer, an agnostic who admits his fear of death, respectfully said, "You're not afraid because you know something I don't know."

Ecclesiastes 3:16–4:3 reveals the need for a God-instructed faith. It depicts the unpleasant side of life: injustice everywhere and the inevitability of death (3:16, 18–21). It expresses that nonbelievers, seeing no reason for hope, must conclude that nonexistence is better than life (3:22–4:3). But it also shows the believer's confidence that God will ultimately make all things right (3:17).

A Bible-instructed faith focuses on Christ—His death, burial, and resurrection (1 Corinthians 15:3–4). Only that kind of faith can bring salvation and comfort. And it gives us confidence that we will spend eternity in heaven.

—Herb Vander Lugt

To put your fears to rest,

put your faith in Christ.

WALK OF FAITH

Read: 2 Corinthians 5:1-11

For we live by faith, not by sight. —2 CORINTHIANS 5:7

Constructed to give people the illusion of walking on air, "The Walk of Faith" is a platform of laminated glass at the top of a 385-foot tower in Blackpool, England. An Associated Press photo showed a woman at the edge of the invisible walkway, fists clenched against her face, trying to summon the courage to take a step. She had been told the platform was safe, but she was still afraid.

Sometimes we feel that way about our circumstances. Perhaps a serious health problem has caused us to question the power and the presence of God.

It's encouraging to note that Paul's familiar words "We live by faith, not by sight" (2 Corinthians 5:7) occur in his discussion about being "away from the body and at home with the Lord" (v. 8). He used a powerful metaphor, calling our body an earthly house that's being destroyed, yet he said we have a heavenly building made by God. He spoke of groaning in our earthly frailty and longing for our heavenly home. He concluded that no matter what circumstances we face, we should make it our goal to please the Lord (v. 9).

Our walk of faith can be challenging and sometimes scary. But because God is powerful and present, we can step out in confidence today.

—*David McCasland*

———

It is better to walk with God by faith than to go alone by sight.

FAITH THAT TAKES ACTION

Read: James 2:14-20

You foolish person, do you want evidence that faith without deeds is useless? —JAMES 2:20

No one can be saved by doing good works. On the other hand, the apostle James taught that faith without works is useless (2:20). To illustrate, he pointed out that faith alone won't feed a hungry person. Only faith that takes action will (vv. 15–16).

How timely this message is! Right now much of our world is suffering a bellyache from not enough food, while countless others have a bellyache from too much.

Tragically, we who have enough to eat often "bellyache" about our food being too done, too tough, too sweet, too cold, or too bland. Then we complain about the dirty dishes that our food creates. A poem from one of my cookbooks turns such ingratitude on its head. Pauline Davis wrote:

Thank God for dirty dishes, they have a story to tell.
While others may be hungry, we are eating very well.
With home, health, and happiness, I shouldn't want to fuss.
By this great stack of evidence, God's been very good to us!

Oh, that we might be grateful, for gratitude is vital to a working faith. People without gratitude seldom care about having a working faith. But believers who are deeply thankful for God's blessings long to share those blessings with others.

Make sure your faith is useful, not useless. And don't neglect the needy, both spiritually and physically, around the world—and around the corner!

—*Joanie Yoder*

Faith always has work to do.

WAITING . . .

Read: Luke 2:22-38

The LORD longs to be gracious to you; therefore he will rise up to show you compassion. For the LORD is a God of justice. Blessed are all who wait for him! —ISAIAH 30:18

Autumn is hunting season here in Michigan. For a few weeks every year, licensed hunters are allowed to go out into the woods and hunt for various species of wildlife. Some hunters build elaborate tree stands high above the ground where they sit quietly for hours waiting for a deer to wander within rifle range.

When I think of hunters who are so patient when it comes to waiting for deer, I think of how impatient we can be when we have to wait for God. We often equate "wait" with "waste." If we're waiting for something (or someone), we think we are doing nothing, which, in an accomplishment-crazed culture, seems like a waste of time.

But waiting serves many purposes. In particular, it proves our faith. Those whose faith is weak are often the first to give up waiting, while those with the strongest faith are willing to wait indefinitely.

When we read the Christmas story in Luke 2, we learn of two people who proved their faith by their willingness to wait. Simeon and Anna waited long, but their time wasn't wasted; it put them in a place where they could witness the coming of Messiah (vv. 22–38).

Not receiving an immediate answer to prayer is no reason to give up faith.

—*Julie Ackerman Link*

Waiting for God is never a waste of time.

THROUGH THE EYES OF FAITH

Read: Luke 2:25-36

"Sovereign Lord, as you have promised, you may now dismiss your servant in peace. For my eyes have seen your salvation." —LUKE 2:29–30

What a touching scene—an aged man holding the baby Jesus in his arms and praising God! (Luke 2:27-32). Simeon had been assured by the Holy Spirit that he would not die until he had seen the promised Messiah, and he came into the temple at the very moment Joseph and Mary entered with the baby Jesus.

I once felt that Simeon was more blessed than I am because he had the privilege of actually touching Jesus, but I must believe without seeing or touching Him. Now I realize that he too had to exercise faith. After all, he was holding in his arms an infant born to a couple he had never met before. His assurance came through the witness of the Holy Spirit in his heart, and we must depend on that same witness today.

Near the end of our Lord's time on earth, when He appeared to His disciples after His resurrection, He said to Thomas, "Because you have seen me, you have believed; blessed are those who have not seen and yet have believed" (John 20:29). We too, through the eyes of faith, can know Christ in a close, personal way.

As we celebrate our Savior, let's pause to look at Him through eyes of faith. When we do, we will be able to lift our voice in praise to God.

—Herb Vander Lugt

Man says that seeing is believing, but God says that believing is seeing.

FEELINGS AND FAITHFULNESS

Read: Psalm 36:5-12

Your love, LORD, reaches to the heavens, your faithfulness to the skies.
—PSALM 36:5

When I was in college, my roommate was engaged to a woman who lived eight hundred miles away. He was a worrier and a pessimist, so he was constantly questioning the closeness of their relationship. He would worry that they were drifting apart. If a day came without a letter, he would convince himself that she didn't love him any longer and was about to break up with him.

I would get so fed up with his worrying that I would insist he call her. He always discovered that nothing had changed and that she was not wavering in her love. Greatly relieved, he would kick himself for having doubted, and he would promise not to worry again—which lasted about three days!

Although we sometimes falter in our faith and question God's love for us, He remains faithful. Even when we doubt His promises or don't feel close to Him or choose to sin, His faithfulness still "reaches to the heavens" (Psalm 36:5). We can be sure God will do all He said He would do (1 Thessalonians 5:24; 2 Thessalonians 3:3). His promises are backed up by His flawless character.

In those times when you don't feel close to God, remind yourself that His feelings for you haven't changed. It's not a matter of how you feel at the moment, but the fact of the rock-solid faithfulness of God.

—David Egner

Trusting God's faithfulness
dispels our fearfulness.

✕

HAPPINESS AND FAITH

Read: Romans 8:29-39

May the God of hope fill you with all joy and peace as you trust in him, so that you may overflow with hope by the power of the Holy Spirit.
—ROMANS 15:13

The chorus of the old hymn "At The Cross" concludes with these cheerful words: "And now I am happy all the day!" I don't know about you, but I can't honestly say that just because I know Jesus as my Savior I'm happy all day. I'm a rather optimistic person and I don't let much get me down, but some circumstances don't warm my heart and make me smile.

Troubles may make us wonder: Isn't our faith supposed to make us happy all the time? Shouldn't Jesus shelter us from harm and danger?

Some people teach these things, but the Bible doesn't. God's Word makes it clear that we will have trouble. In Romans 8, for example, the apostle Paul talked frankly about tough times we could face (vv. 35–39). The fact is, Jesus doesn't protect us from all trouble, but His love and His companionship guide us as we go through it.

A more realistic attitude than being "happy all the day" is one stated by a Christian who said, "Now that I'm saved, I'm happier when I am down than I was when I was happy before I was saved."

With Jesus Christ, we can have real joy and make it through even the bad times.

—*Dave Branon*

Happiness depends on happenings, but joy depends on Jesus.

TRUE FAITH

Read: Romans 10:1-13

God made him who had no sin to be sin for us, so that in him we might become the righteousness of God. —2 CORINTHIANS 5:21

Some things in life call for us to be absolutely accurate—to do exactly as the directions say. For instance, I can't fill out my tax returns any old way I want. I have to do exactly as the tax code requires, or I'll spend a lot of time explaining myself. Even in a land of liberty, we are bound to follow certain rules.

Adhering to the Bible as the guidebook in our spiritual life is even more vital. Some people may consider these matters to be peripheral and easily ignored, but we must get them right.

That's why it is distressing to learn that according to the Barna Research Group, 42 percent of Americans think Jesus committed sins. And even 25 percent of professing Christians say He was not sinless. Beyond that, 61 percent of Americans think there are other ways to salvation besides faith in Christ.

These are dangerous deviations from the truth. Our Guidebook, the Bible, is clear—Jesus Christ lived a perfect life, and His sacrificial death is the only way to establish a relationship with God.

We can't afford to make up our own rules. Only those who call "on the name of the Lord will be saved" (Romans 10:13). That's true faith. Any other way leads to eternal death.

—*Dave Branon*

To get into heaven, it's who you know that counts.

UNEXPECTED BLESSINGS

Read: Ruth 2:11-23

He will renew your life and sustain you in your old age.
For your daughter-in-law, who loves you and who is better to you
than seven sons, has given him birth. —RUTH 4:15

Naomi and Ruth came together in less-than-ideal circumstances. To escape a famine in Israel, Naomi's family moved to Moab. While living there, her two sons married Moabite women: Orpah and Ruth. Then Naomi's husband and sons died. In that culture, women were dependent on men, which left the three widows in a predicament.

Word came to Naomi that the famine in Israel had ended, so she decided to make the long trek home. Orpah and Ruth started to go with her, but Naomi urged them to return home, saying, "The LORD's hand has turned against me!" (1:13).

Orpah went home, but Ruth continued, affirming her belief in Naomi's God despite Naomi's own fragile faith (1:15–18).

The story started in desperately unpleasant circumstances: famine, death, and despair (1:1–5). It changed direction due to undeserved kindnesses: Ruth to Naomi (1:16-17; 2:11–12) and Boaz to Ruth (2:13–14).

It involved unlikely people: two widows (an aging Jew and a young Gentile) and Boaz, the son of a prostitute (Joshua 2:1; Matthew 1:5).

It depended on unexplainable intervention: Ruth just so "happened" to glean in the field of Boaz (2:3).

And it ended in unimaginable blessing: a baby who would be in the lineage of the Messiah (4:16–17).

God makes miracles out of what seems insignificant: fragile faith, a little kindness, and ordinary people.

—Julie Ackerman Link

In all the setbacks of your life as a believer, God is plotting for your joy. —John Piper

FEAR AND FAITH

Read: Matthew 8:18-27

When I am afraid, I put my trust in you. —PSALM 56:3

I agree with the statement "Faith chases out fear, or fear chases out faith." But I also know that no believer is immune to panic or terror.

One Sunday evening the hair on my neck stood up and my heart rate soared as the driver of an oncoming car tried to pass another vehicle when he shouldn't have, and I was forced off the road.

Christians caught in a major earthquake have told me about the panic that seized them when it occurred.

Military people who have survived intense bombing attacks say that anyone who claims he wasn't afraid at the time is either a liar or a fool.

It is not a sin to feel panic or terror in a life-threatening situation.

During a sudden, violent storm, the disciples were gently rebuked as having "little faith" because they should have known that nothing could harm them while Jesus was in their boat. But they did the right thing in calling out to Him, "Lord, save us!" (Matthew 8:25).

When fear strikes, think of God and consciously trust Him. The psalmist said, "When I am afraid, I put my trust in [God]" (Psalm 56:3).

Remember, fear will chase out faith, or faith will chase out fear.

—Herb Vander Lugt

Faith can break the stranglehold of fear.

"MOWER" FAITH

Read: Genesis 24:10-28

Then [Abraham's servant] prayed, "LORD, God of my master Abraham, make me successful today, and show kindness to my master Abraham."
—GENESIS 24:12

The fifth-grader watched her father struggling under the hot sun to cut the grass on the family's sizable yard. When he was finally done, she said to him, "Daddy, I wish we had a riding lawn mower. I'm going to buy you one." She did more than make what seemed like an impossible promise. She began praying for a riding mower for her dad. And she began doing odd jobs to earn money.

Finally the girl had saved up $50, but everyone knew that wasn't enough. Then one day she and her mom saw a riding mower that was for sale. Skeptically, they took a closer look at the sign. They couldn't believe their eyes: $50. And the mower worked!

In Genesis 24, we read the account of Abraham's servant seeking a bride for Isaac. He had the difficult task of finding a woman from a family hundreds of miles away. And she had to be willing to return with him to Canaan. He prayed specifically, did everything he could, and waited on the Lord.

Two seemingly impossible requests. Two faithful believers in prayer and action. It's a formula for great results.

Not all prayers are answered affirmatively, of course, but that isn't our concern. Our job is to see the need, ask God for help, and do what we can. We all need "mower" faith.

—*Dave Branon*

A living faith is a working faith.

✕

JESUS, MAN OF FAITH

Read: John 11:1-15

When he heard this, Jesus said, "This sickness will not end in death.
No, it is for God's glory so that God's Son may be glorified through it."
—JOHN 11:4

Jesus laid aside the privileges and glory of His deity when He became a man. As a result, He had to face life's trials and tests just as we do (Philippians 2:5–8). Like us, He had to exercise trust in God His Father.

I see this in the story about Lazarus. Jesus deliberately delayed departing for Bethany when He heard that Lazarus was sick. By waiting, He was exercising faith in His Father's wisdom and power. He knew it was His Father's will that Lazarus die so that God would be glorified (John 11:4).

Because of His faith, Jesus returned to a place where an attempt had been made on His life (v. 8). And even though He had never restored to life a person who had been buried, He declared confidently, "I am going there to wake him up" (v. 11).

His disciples might have wondered why Jesus didn't heal Lazarus before he died. Why go into dangerous territory when He had the power to perform miracles from a distance? (Matthew 8:5–13). But Jesus didn't question His Father's leading. He went forward with perfect trust in His wisdom.

Although we may not see clearly the end result of the trials we face, we can have confident faith in our heavenly Father. We can trust God to glorify himself and to work out His good purposes through us.

—*Herb Vander Lugt*

Faith focuses on God instead of life's problems.

SMALL FAITH IN A BIG GOD

Read: Matthew 17:14–21

He replied, "Because you have so little faith. Truly I tell you, if you have faith as small as a mustard seed, you can say to this mountain, 'Move from here to there,' and it will move. Nothing will be impossible for you."
—MATTHEW 17:20

Faith—we all wish we had more of it, especially when facing mountainous problems. Yet most of us are well practiced in faith. We sit down in chairs without checking them out; we use microwave ovens without analyzing how they work; we put keys in doors and expect them to open. We don't go around moaning, "If only I had more faith in chairs, in microwaves, in keys." We depend on these objects because we see them as reliable— not because we've worked up great feelings of confidence.

Jesus didn't say to His disciples, "Have more faith in God." He simply said, "Have faith in God" (Mark 11:22).

Bible teacher Stuart Briscoe writes, "Faith is only as valid as its object. You could have tremendous faith in very thin ice and drown . . . . You could have very little faith in very thick ice and be perfectly secure."

Many Christians have faith in faith rather than faith in God. When facing trials, they agonize to attain mountain-size faith. But Jesus taught that faith the size of a mustard seed is sufficient—if planted in the soil of God's greatness.

What is your mountain today? As soon as you plant your mustard seed of faith in God, your mountain becomes His responsibility—and you can rest in His faithfulness.

—*Joanie Yoder*

Have faith in God—not faith in faith.

WHY KEEP THE FAITH?

Read: 2 Timothy 3

But as for you, continue in what you have learned and have become convinced of, because you know those from whom you learned it.
—2 TIMOTHY 3:14

Many Christians are on the front lines of some very important battles. Some are speaking out on social issues and moral decline. Others are helping to relieve suffering and battling the effects of poverty. Still others are trying to make a difference in government or entertainment.

Sometimes these battles are won, but often the other side gains ground. It can be a discouraging effort.

When we lose a skirmish on the front lines of today's battles, how does that affect us? We may feel discouraged, but we need not feel hopeless. We know Christ will win ultimately, and we can be encouraged because there are some things that cannot be taken away from us:

- Jesus Christ's continual presence with us (Hebrews 13:5).
- The Lord's promise of eternal life (Titus 1:2).
- The Holy Spirit's indwelling (1 Corinthians 6:19).
- Access to our heavenly Father through prayer (Ephesians 2:18).
- Spiritual gifts to serve the body of Christ (1 Corinthians 12).

It hurts to lose a battle in the daily fight for what is right. But as Paul made clear in 2 Timothy 3, it should come as no surprise. We are called only to be faithful. And when we contemplate what Christ has given to us, we'll never have to wonder why we should keep the faith.

—*Dave Branon*

Having the Holy Spirit on the inside prepares you for any battle on the outside.

FOR SINNERS ONLY

Read: Romans 3:19-31

This righteousness is given through faith in Jesus Christ to all who believe. There is no difference between Jew and Gentile, for all have sinned and fall short of the glory of God. —ROMANS 3:22-23

It's heartbreaking to realize that the majority of people in our world are spiritually lost and without Christ. Among them are the lovely and unlovely, the caring and uncaring, the eloquent and the crude. As we witness for Christ, we may wrongly assume that people with social graces are closer to God's kingdom.

However, pleasant people need Christ just as much as unpleasant ones because no one has a spiritual advantage when it comes to salvation. Paul explained why in Romans 3: "There is no difference . . . for all have sinned and fall short of the glory of God . . . . For we maintain that a person is justified by faith apart from the works of the law" (vv. 22–23, 28).

Yes, salvation is God's free gift to sinners. And since all of us are sinners, the only "contribution" we make toward our salvation is the sin from which we need to be saved! Oswald Chambers said that the only way a person can be born again is to renounce all good. He wrote, "Any coward among us will give up wrong things, but will he give up right things?" We cannot rely on our own natural goodness.

We need to share with all kinds of people the salvation Christ offers, for as the apostle Paul said, "There is no difference."

—*Joanie Yoder*

You can never speak to the wrong person about Christ.

FAITH AND THE IMPOSSIBLE

Read: Matthew 1:18-25

When Joseph woke up, he did what the angel of the Lord had commanded him and took Mary home as his wife. —MATTHEW 1:24

A minister told me he can't believe that Mary was a virgin when she gave birth to Jesus. He said, "In our enlightened age, we know that a miracle like a virgin birth is contrary to the course of nature." He dismissed the gospel accounts as the imagination of writers who lacked the insights of modern science.

I said to him, "Granted, we have come a long way in scientific knowledge since the first century. But I think Joseph and the men who wrote the New Testament knew perfectly well what it takes to produce a baby. The fact of the matter is that Joseph lost his confidence in Mary's fidelity to him when he learned that she was pregnant. He was ready to break their engagement. But the angel of the Lord assured him that the conception came about by the Holy Spirit."

Unless we are willing to believe in miracles, we will miss the true meaning of Christ's birth—that the infinite God who created and upholds everything compressed himself into a tiny baby. That is a miracle beyond comprehension! If we don't believe that happened, we will remain in spiritual darkness. On the other hand, if we believe it, the idea that Jesus was born of a virgin mother will be easy to accept. We will have the faith to believe the impossible.

—*Herb Vander Lugt*

Believe in God and you'll believe in miracles; believe in His Son and you'll experience one.

FAITH TO OBEY

Read: Jeremiah 32:1-9; 16-25

"Then, just as the LORD had said, my cousin Hanamel came to me in the courtyard of the guard and said, 'Buy my field at Anathoth in the territory of Benjamin. Since it is your right to redeem it and possess it, buy it for yourself.' I knew that this was the word of the LORD; so I bought the field at Anathoth from my cousin Hanamel and weighed out for him seventeen shekels of silver." —JEREMIAH 32:8–9

A woman was married to a successful young businessman. He had a good reputation and an excellent income. Then he sensed that God was calling him to sell his business, go to Bible school, and enter missionary service. To his wife, it seemed foolish to give up so much. Yet she believed God wanted her to follow her husband's lead. She struggled within herself—but found the faith to obey. Today they are experiencing God's blessing as he uses his skills in Brazil.

In our Bible reading today, Jeremiah bought a piece of real estate from his cousin Hanamel while Jerusalem was under siege. Jeremiah purchased the field even though he had already prophesied that the city was going to fall. This didn't make sense. Why buy property in a land that was about to be occupied by the enemy? Because God had told him to. The Lord used this incident to dramatize His promise that Israel would again possess the land (v. 15).

We need that same willingness to obey the Lord even if it doesn't seem to make sense. If He gives a command, our part is to believe Him and carry it out.

The issue may not be as dramatic for us. Sometimes it may seem pointless to be honest instead of deceitful, or to forgive rather than hold a grudge. But whatever God calls us to do, we need the faith to obey.

—David Egner

Understanding can wait, obedience cannot.

FAITH IN THE FACTS

Read: Hebrews 11:1-6

Now faith is confidence in what we hope for and assurance about what we do not see. —HEBREWS 11:1

On December 17, 1903, Orville and Wilbur Wright made history. Their motorized vehicle defied the law of gravity and flew through the air. The idea wasn't new. Years before the Wright brothers got off the ground at Kitty Hawk, mathematicians and scientists had proven that flight was possible. But many people who read those facts couldn't believe that flying would ever become a reality. The Wright brothers believed the facts and mathematical formulas, and they built the first flying machine. When it became airborne, they demonstrated that you have to trust in the facts and act on them if you want results.

There's a parallel here to the spiritual life of everyone who has heard the gospel of Jesus Christ. Many people know that He died on the cross for their sins and rose from the grave, but they will not act on this knowledge. They are like those who knew the mathematical facts and formulas about flight but had no faith in them.

God has made the facts clear. He has provided for our salvation through the substitutionary death of His Son. But many people who are aware of this are still lost. They know all about Christ, but they have never put their faith in Him. If that describes you, don't delay any longer. Believe in Jesus today.

—*Paul Van Gorder*

Unless you believe, you will not understand. —Augustine

THE FRIENDLY SKIES OF FAITH

Read: Luke 17:3-10

The apostles said to the Lord, "Increase our faith!" —LUKE 17:5

Millions of people are afraid to travel by air. Many of them know very well what the statistics say—that they are safer in an airplane than in the family car or the bathtub. But that doesn't matter. Researchers say that a conscious fear of crashing is usually not the problem. Instead, at the root of their anxiety is the fear that once they leave the ground they will lose control of their lives.

A similar crisis of faith occurs when a person puts himself in the care of God. He too is carried a long way from what the world considers "solid ground." Trusting an invisible Lord can be frightening, especially for a new Christian.

Jesus's disciples expressed their concern when He told them that they would have to rise to levels of forgiveness and mercy previously unknown to them. Yet He responded to their lack of faith by pointing out that it takes only a small amount of obedient trust in Him to put the power of heaven at their disposal.

That's the key to our journey through life. When we learn what Christ wants from us, we must take the first step of obedience. He will then give us the strength to do what He wants us to do.

Lord, increase our faith.

—*Mart DeHaan*

———

A little faith can lift you above your fears.

WHO'S GOING TO HEAVEN?

Read: Romans 3:21–28

For we maintain that a person is justified by faith apart from the works of the law. —ROMANS 3:28

A poll for *U.S. News & World Report* asked 1,000 adults their opinion about who would likely make it into heaven. At the top of that list, to no one's surprise, was a well-known religious figure. Several celebrities were also listed. But it was surprising to me that of the people being surveyed, 87 percent thought they themselves were likely to get into heaven.

I can't help but wonder what qualifications for admission into heaven they had in mind. People have many erroneous ideas about what God requires.

Is it virtuous character? Giving generous contributions to deserving charities? Following an orthodox creed? Attending church and being involved in religious activities? Commendable as these qualities may be, they miss by an eternity the one thing God requires for entrance into heaven—a personal commitment to Jesus Christ as Savior and Lord (John 1:12; 1 Timothy 2:5). Although faith in Jesus will no doubt be seen in a person's actions (James 2:14–20), charitable living or religious activity is not a substitute for trusting in Jesus's sacrificial death for our sin.

Are you confident that you're headed for heaven? You can be—but only if you're trusting in Jesus.

—*Vernon Grounds*

Jesus took our place on the cross to give us a place in heaven.

IT'S TOO EASY

Read: Romans 4:1-8

*To the one who does not work but trusts God who justifies the ungodly,
their faith is credited as righteousness.* —ROMANS 4:5

I read about an instant cake mix that was a big flop. The instructions said all you had to do was add water and bake. The company couldn't understand why it didn't sell—until their research discovered that the buying public felt uneasy about a mix that required only water. People thought it was too easy. So the company altered the formula and changed the directions to call for adding an egg to the mix in addition to the water. The idea worked, and sales jumped dramatically.

That story reminds me of how some people react to the plan of salvation. To them it sounds too easy and simple to be true, even though the Bible says, "By grace you have been saved, through faith, . . . it is the gift of God—not by works" (Ephesians 2:8–9). They feel that there is something more they must do, something they must add to God's "recipe" for salvation. They think they must perform good works to gain God's favor and earn eternal life. But the Bible is clear—we are saved "not because of righteous things we had done, but because of his mercy" (Titus 3:5).

Unlike the cake-mix manufacturer, God has not changed His "formula" to make salvation more marketable. The gospel we proclaim must be free of works, even though it may sound too easy.

—*Richard DeHaan*

We are saved by God's mercy, not by our merit—by Christ's dying, not by our doing.

✗

A GOOD STRETCH

Read: Romans 8:26-28

*But [the Lord] said to me, "My grace is sufficient for you, for my power is made perfect in weakness." —*2 CORINTHIANS 12:9

Physical therapy is a painful necessity after knee-replacement surgery. Part of my routine involved my therapist pulling my knee back into a bent position and holding it taut. "Good stretch?" Mason would ask encouragingly. "No," I winced, "not that good!"

I soon learned, however, how important it is to stretch one's muscles and joints—sometimes causing discomfort—to regain full range of motion.

That wasn't the first time I've been "stretched" outside my comfort zone. God has sometimes urged me to share my faith with someone I didn't know very well, to give an offering that was far beyond what I usually give, or to confront someone about a situation.

Abraham's life illustrates the importance of faith when God asks us to move beyond our comfort zone. "By faith Abraham, when called . . . obeyed and went, even though he did not know where he was going" (Hebrews 11:8).

When we stretch our spiritual muscles, we may feel discomfort. But God assures us, "My grace is sufficient for you, for my power is made perfect in weakness" (2 Corinthians 12:9). Our adequacy—our sufficiency—is found in Him (3:5).

When you boldly step out in faith and obedience to God, you may be surprised at how a "good stretch" can strengthen your spiritual life!

—*Cindy Hess Kasper*

Our faith is stretched by exchanging our weakness for God's strength.

THE COMEBACK KING

Read: John 14:1-6

Before long, the world will not see me anymore, but you will see me.
Because I live, you also will live. —JOHN 14:19

We admire anyone who makes a comeback after failure and defeat. Several years ago, *Sports Illustrated* magazine featured an article on the greatest comebacks of all time. Surprisingly, they selected the resurrection of Jesus as number one. It was stated this way: "Jesus Christ, 33 AD. Defies critics and stuns the Romans with His resurrection."

How discerning! In any list of history's comebacks, Jesus's victory over the grave surely merits first place. Indeed, His resurrection is in a class that soars above any other comeback.

Death ultimately triumphs over life. When a person dies, there is no possibility of renewed existence—at least not in this world. But that wasn't so with Jesus. He had promised His disciples that after being crucified by His enemies, He would come back to life—triumphing over the grave. Matthew records this in his gospel: "Jesus began to explain to his disciples that he must go to Jerusalem and suffer many things . . . be killed and on the third day be raised to life" (16:21). And that is what happened to our Savior.

Jesus Christ's comeback assures us that we too by faith in Him will come back when we are resurrected from the grave (John 11:25–26).

—*Vernon Grounds*

———

The empty tomb is the foundation of our faith.

UNOPENED TOMORROWS

Read: Matthew 6:25-34

For we live by faith, not by sight. —2 CORINTHIANS 5:7

We often wish we could see what lies around the corner in life. Then we could prepare for it, control it, or avoid it.

A wise person has said, "Though we can't see around corners, God can." How much better and more reassuring that is!

One day my ten-year-old granddaughter Emily and I were boiling eggs for breakfast. As we stared into the boiling water and wondered how long it would take to get the eggs just right, Emily said, "Pity we can't open them up to see how they're doing." I agreed. But that would have spoiled them, so we had to rely on guesswork, with no guarantee of results.

We began talking about other things we would like to see but can't—like tomorrow. Too bad we can't crack tomorrow open, we said, to see if it's the way we would like it. But meddling with tomorrow before its time, like opening a partly cooked egg, would spoil both today and tomorrow.

Because Jesus has promised to care for us every day—and that includes tomorrow—we can live by faith one day at a time (Matthew 6:33–34).

Emily and I decided to leave tomorrow safely in God's hands. Have you?

—*Joanie Yoder*

You're only cooking up trouble when you stew about tomorrow.

THE ADVENTURE

Read: Esther 4:13-17

Who knows but that you have come to your royal position for such a time as this? —ESTHER 4:14

When I was about seven, I was in the car with my mom and two sisters when my mother pulled over to the side of the road to study the map. "Are we lost, Mom?" I was worried.

"Oh, no," she replied cheerfully, quickly folding up the map. "We're on an adventure." My sisters and I exchanged doubtful glances as one of them whispered knowingly, "We're lost."

Adventures can be fun—and scary. They usually involve a bit of the unknown. As we walk in fellowship with God, it's likely that our lives will have many unique adventures—opportunities to serve Him. If we're reluctant or scared and we turn down an opportunity, we miss out. Will God still get the job done? Of course. But someone else will receive the blessing.

In Esther 4, Mordecai encouraged the young Queen Esther to help rescue her people. He cautioned: "If you remain completely silent . . . deliverance will arise for the Jews from another place, but you and your father's house will perish. Yet who knows whether you have come to the kingdom for such a time as this?" (v. 14 NKJV).

Esther was naturally frightened to take this assignment. But God used her courage and faith to deliver her people. Trust God to show you the way. Adventure ahead!

—*Cindy Hess Kasper*

———

Courage is fear that has said its prayers.

UNLIKELY HEROES

Read: Judges 2:7-19

Then the LORD raised up judges, who saved them out of the hands of these raiders. —JUDGES 2:16

The book of Judges is an account of God's people descending into spiritual indifference and rebellion. After the death of Joshua and his peers, the next generation "forsook the LORD, the God of their ancestors, . . . They followed and worshiped various gods of the peoples around them" (Judges 2:12).

This dismal record of wavering allegiance hardly seems the place to find spiritual heroes, yet four people from Judges—Gideon, Barak, Samson, and Jephthah (chapters 4–16)—are named in the New Testament book of Hebrews (11:32). Along with Noah, Abraham, Moses, and other notables, they are commended for their faith.

Judges, however, presents these men as flawed people who nevertheless responded to God's call during a time of spiritual darkness in their culture. The Bible honors them for their faith, not for their perfection. They were recipients of God's grace as surely as we are.

In every generation, God raises up people who are true to Him and to His Word. The measure of their lives and of ours is not the absence of failure but the presence of God's gracious forgiveness and the faith to obey His call. All of God's champions are unlikely heroes.

—*David McCasland*

Faith in Christ can make extraordinary heroes out of ordinary people.

SMART ARMOR SYSTEM

Read: Ephesians 6:10-18

Take up the shield of faith, with which you can extinguish all the flaming arrows of the evil one. —EPHESIANS 6:16

United States Army and Pentagon officials have developed a sophisticated armor system to protect tanks against enemy fire. According to the *Army Times,* this system protects armored vehicles against some of the most deadly armor piercing rockets. The Smart Armor System keeps these missiles from penetrating the armor of tanks because special reactive tiles will deflect them.

As followers of Jesus Christ, we need protection from the "fiery darts" being hurled at us by Satan. He has some powerful missiles that can stir up within us doubt, fear, disappointment, impurity, lust, greed, selfishness, covetousness, and pride. And he attacks us when we are most vulnerable in these areas. But God has given us the shield of faith for our protection to deflect Satan's most powerful missiles. When we trust God, believing what He tells us in His Word, the enemy's most deadly attacks will be futile.

As you go out into battle today, put on the whole armor of God. Above all, take up the shield of faith. Reassert your trust in God and commit your ways to Him. It's your Smart Armor System.

—*David Egner*

Trust in God's Word is a sure defense against temptation.

ALL SAFE! ALL WELL!

Read: Hebrews 11:8-16

Now faith is confidence in what we hope for and assurance about what we do not see. —HEBREWS 11:1

In January 1915, the ship *Endurance* was trapped and crushed in the ice off the coast of Antarctica. The group of polar explorers, led by Ernest Shackleton, survived and managed to reach Elephant Island in three small lifeboats. Trapped on this uninhabited island, far from normal shipping lanes, they had one hope. On April 24, 1916, twenty-two men watched as Shackleton and five comrades set out in a tiny lifeboat for South Georgia, an island eight hundred miles away. The odds seemed impossible, and if they failed, they would all certainly die. What joy, then, when more than *four months* later a boat appeared on the horizon with Shackleton on its bow shouting, "Are you all well?" And the call came back, "All safe! All well!"

What held those men together and kept them alive over those months? Faith and hope placed in one man. They believed that Shackleton would find a way to save them.

This human example of faith and hope echoes the faith of the heroes listed in Hebrews 11. Their faith in the "substance of things hoped for, the evidence of things not seen" kept them going through great difficulties and trials (Hebrews 11:1 NKJV).

As we look out upon the horizon of our own problems, may we not despair. May we have hope through the certainty of our faith in the One Man—Jesus, our God and Savior.

—*Randy Kilgore*

The hope of Jesus shines brightly even on our darkest day.

MAGIC EYE

Read: Hebrews 11:1-10

*Without faith it is impossible to please God, because anyone
who comes to him must believe that he exists and that he rewards
those who earnestly seek him.* —HEBREWS 11:6

One of my nephews brought a book of Magic Eye images to
a family gathering. Magic Eye images look like ordinary two-
dimensional patterns, but when viewed in a certain way, the
flat surface appears three-dimensional.

We took turns trying to train our eyes to make the three-
dimensional image pop out. One family member had trouble
seeing the extra dimension. Several times I noticed he had the
book open, looking at it from all different distances and directions. But even though he couldn't see the hidden image, he
believed it was there because others had seen it.

His persistence made me think about the importance of
having the same tenacity in matters of faith. The danger for
those who doubt is that they stop looking for God because
they believe He can't be found. Moses warned the Israelites
that future generations would wander from God. He promised, however, that those who seek God with all their heart
and soul would find Him (Deuteronomy 4:29). The book of
Hebrews confirms that God rewards those who diligently seek
Him (11:6).

If you struggle to believe, remember: Just because you don't
see God doesn't mean He doesn't exist. He promises to be
found by those who seek Him.

—*Julie Ackerman Link*

Because God is great, He will be sought; because God is good,
He will be found.

THE RIGHT KIND OF FAITH

Read: Hebrews 11:1-7

Without faith it is impossible to please God, because anyone who comes to him must believe that he exists and that he rewards those who earnestly seek him. —HEBREWS 11:6

Everybody has faith. Some people say they don't need it, but they are wrong. I recall a fellow soldier who said to me one day, "I believe in nothing I can't see, and I can handle everything I can see." I asked him, "You don't believe in the existence of viruses and atoms, in goodness and badness?" He hemmed and hawed and then reluctantly admitted he did exercise some faith. The issue, then, is not whether I have faith, but is it reasonable? And does it meet my deepest needs?

I'm convinced that the Christian faith adequately answers both of these questions. It begins with God as Creator. This premise makes more sense than believing that matter is eternal and that life evolved from it. The chances of life beginning through a series of accidents is about the same as a dictionary coming into existence through an explosion in a print shop. But what about the second question? Does the Christian faith meet our deepest needs? Indeed it does! It fills life with meaning, it provides forgiveness, it brings power to overcome sinful habits, and it gives hope. No man-made religion or atheistic philosophy can do all this.

If you have never accepted Jesus Christ as your Savior, you have the wrong kind of faith. By an act of trust, acknowledge that there is a God. Admit that you've sinned, and ask Jesus to save you. Then make it your aim to obey Him. You'll soon know for sure that you have the right kind of faith.

—*Herb Vander Lugt*

Christian faith is both assuring and enduring.

FORECAST OF FAITH

Read: Psalm 77:1-15

Then I thought, "To this I will appeal: the years when the Most High stretched out his right hand." —PSALM 77:10

Are you about to lose your faith? Don't give up yet. Remember the author Psalm 77? He had sunk so low that all hope seemed gone. He was so troubled he couldn't sleep. He was so depressed he couldn't even talk about it. That's what he was— depressed! Down! Blue! He was so low that the fleas of the field had to get on their knees to bite him. But then something happened. He thought how his forefathers had gone through similar troubles before the Lord delivered them, and his faith was renewed.

Looking back can restore hope and give us reason to look ahead. Let me illustrate. After a long and hard winter, the bright and balmy days of spring are suddenly invaded by a renegade polar air mass. You think winter is starting all over again. Cabin-fevered housewives start to panic. Shovel-worn men slump back into their chairs and begin to worry about the impact of the storm on the heating bill. But nobody concludes that the age-old order of the seasons has come to an abrupt end, or that the solar system has reversed its cycle. Looking back reminds you that late-season storms have happened before and reassures you that spring will come.

So too, the Bible shows us that men and women of God have seen hard times before. It reminds us that many times the sky has been dark and cold just before the Lord responded with the warmth and power of His love.

So don't give up yet. Look back. Then look ahead. The people of God have walked this way before. The forecast of faith is always bright.

—*Mart DeHaan*

Do not judge God's love by
His providences but by His promises.

✕

NOTHING FOR SOMETHING

Read: Romans 4:1-8

*To the one who does not work but trusts God who justifies the ungodly,
their faith is credited as righteousness.* —ROMANS 4:5

If you're looking for a great deal, you'll want to carefully examine the ad for a national donut store chain:

Free! Three muffins when you buy three at the regular half-dozen price.

If that rather confusing statement means you can buy six muffins for the price of six, it's not exactly a bargain!

So many of the seemingly great buys in our world are like deceptive advertisements. You end up receiving nothing for something, when you thought it would be the other way around.

Think about it in spiritual terms. Various religions require a long list of activities in exchange for what amounts to hopelessness.

One religion, for example, expects its adherents to eat only leftovers, never injure a living thing, and denounce all preferences of sounds, colors, smells, and people. In return for all this meaningless (and impossible) self-denial, the individual hopes to be reincarnated to a better life.

In reality, spiritual rewards are God's to give, and He does so on the basis of His grace. Only God's plan of salvation offers something that is truly free (Romans 4:5). Jesus paid the price for our redemption; all He asks is that we put our faith in Him. Any other plan is nothing for something.

—*Dave Branon*

If we could earn our salvation, Christ would not have died to provide it.

BABY STEPS

Read: Psalm 18:31-36

He makes my feet like the feet of a deer; he causes me to stand on the heights. —PSALM 18:33

My baby is learning to walk. I have to hold her, and she clings to my fingers because she is still unsteady on her feet. She is afraid of slipping, but I'm there to steady her and watch over her. As she walks with my help, her eyes sparkle with gratitude, happiness, and security. But sometimes she cries when I don't let her take dangerous paths, not realizing that I am protecting her.

Like my baby girl, we often need someone to watch over us, to guide and steady us in our spiritual walk. And we have that someone—God our Father—who helps His children learn to walk, guides our steps, holds our hand, and keeps us on the right path.

King David knew all about the need for God's watchful care in his life. In Psalm 18 he describes how God gives us strength and guidance when we are lost or confused (v. 32). He keeps our feet steady, like the feet of the deer that can climb high places without slipping (v. 33). And if we do slip, His hand is there for us (v. 35).

Whether we are new believers just learning to walk in the faith or we are further along in our walk with God, all of us need His guiding, steadying hand.

—*Keila Ochoa*

God watches over me every step of the way.

FASHION OR FAITH?

Read: 1 Corinthians 1:18–25

May I never boast except in the cross of our Lord Jesus Christ,
through which the world has been crucified to me, and I to the world.
—GALATIANS 6:14

Os Guinness tells of a Jewish man, imprisoned fifteen years by Soviet authorities for political dissidence, who became a Christian while in the terrible Gulag. He was sustained throughout that long ordeal by his faith in the Savior and by the memory of his four-year-old son he hoped to see again one day.

When he was finally released, the man anticipated the reunion with heart-pounding excitement. How thrilled he was to notice as they hugged each other that his son was wearing a cross!

After they had talked about many things, he asked his son, who was then nineteen years old, just what the cross meant to him. His heart was crushed by the answer: "Father, for my generation the cross is just a fashion statement."

The apostle Paul saw the cross as a symbol of the very core of his faith. It bore witness to his radically transformed life. He testified, "May I never boast except in the cross of our Lord Jesus Christ, through which the world has been crucified to me, and I to the world" (Galatians 6:14).

What about you? Is the cross just a fashion statement? Or does it inspire you to echo Paul's heartfelt boast in the death and resurrection of the Lord Jesus Christ?

—*Vernon Grounds*

If you wear the cross, think of the Christ of the cross.

NO CHANGE

Read: Romans 4:1-12

Since we have been justified through faith, we have peace with God through our Lord Jesus Christ. —ROMANS 5:1

All around us, life is changing at a dizzying pace. Even in the church, change is happening so fast that it can be tough to keep up.

For example, to communicate more effectively with people, Christians have changed the way "church" is done. Many believers have become accustomed to churches without pews, sanctuaries without hymnbooks, and message outlines and songs projected onto large screens.

Christians have also recognized the need to change their methods of reaching out to non-Christians with the gospel of Jesus. Churches use sports leagues to bring the gospel to people in their neighborhood. They open up food pantries to reach out to the disadvantaged. They hold special group meetings for people dealing with grief or addictions.

Not everything is changing, however. Dr. M. R. DeHaan wrote in the first edition of *Our Daily Bread* in 1956: "If there is one thing Paul insisted upon, it is that works have nothing to do with obtaining or retaining our salvation. We are justified by faith, and faith alone" (Romans 4:5; 5:1).

Modes and methods of worship may change. But salvation is through faith in Jesus alone. That will never change—ever.

—*Dave Branon*

In a world of constant change, you can trust God's unchanging Word.

DEGREES OF FAITH

Read: Luke 7:1-10

Then he touched their eyes and said, "According to your faith let it be done to you." —MATTHEW 9:29

Not all Christians exercise the same degree of faith. Some people seem to think their problem is too big for God to solve. Others are sure that God is all-powerful, but they're not confident that He will do what is best for them. Still others affirm, "I know what God can do, and I'll trust Him to do what He has promised." These various attitudes range from a weak and tentative faith to a firm confidence that takes God at His word and believes He is good.

As we study the ministry of Jesus, we see varying degrees of faith in those who came to Him. He cast out a mute spirit from a son whose father wavered between faith and doubt (Mark 9:17–24). He healed a leper who knew He could but was not sure He would (Mark 1:40–45). And He healed the servant of a centurion who was so sure of the outcome that he asked Jesus merely to speak the word from afar (Luke 7:1–10).

These examples don't teach that God always answers according to the strength of our faith. Rather, in His wisdom He responds to any degree of faith. His ultimate goal is to lead us to trust Him completely. Because of who Jesus is, He can turn the weakest faith into strong faith.

—*Dennis DeHaan*

Our faith in God grows greater as we recognize the greatness of our God.

𝓧

THE BABEL PROJECT

Read: Genesis 11:1-9

Unless the LORD builds the house, the builders labor in vain.
Unless the LORD watches over the city, the guards stand watch in vain.
—PSALM 127:1

Two workmen were asked what they were building together. One said he was building a garage. The other replied that he was building a cathedral. A day later there was only one man laying bricks. When asked where the second was, the first replied, "Oh, he got fired. He insisted on building a cathedral instead of a garage."

Something similar happened on the ancient worksite of Babel. A group of people decided they would build a city and a tower that would reach to the heavens and unite their world (Genesis 11:4). But God didn't want them working on a grand, self-centered plan based on the idea that they could rise to the heights of God and solve all of their own problems. So He came down, stopped the project, scattered the people "over the face of the whole earth," and gave them different languages (vv. 8–9).

God wanted people to see Him as the solution to their problems, and He revealed His plan for them to Abraham (12:1–3). Through the faith of Abraham and his descendants, He would show the world how to look for a city "whose architect and builder is God" (Hebrews 11:8–10).

Our faith does not rise out of our own dreams and solutions. The foundation of faith is in God alone and what He can do in and through us.

—*Mart DeHaan*

God wants to do what only He can do in and for us.

BRINGING OUR FRIENDS TO JESUS

Read: Mark 2:1–12

When Jesus saw their faith, he said to the paralyzed man,
"Son, your sins are forgiven." —MARK 2:5

During my childhood, one of the most feared diseases was polio, often called "infantile paralysis" because most of those infected were young children. Before a preventive vaccine was developed in the mid-1950s, some 20,000 people were paralyzed by polio, and about 1,000 died from it each year in the United States alone.

In ancient times, paralysis was viewed as a permanent, hopeless condition. But one group of men believed Jesus could help their paralyzed friend. While Jesus was teaching in the village of Capernaum, four men carried the man to Him. When they couldn't reach Jesus because of the crowd, "they made an opening in the roof above Jesus by digging through it and then lowered the mat the man was lying on" (Mark 2:1–4).

"When Jesus saw their faith, he said to the paralyzed man, 'Son, your sins are forgiven' " (v. 5), followed by "Get up, take your mat and go home" (v. 11). How remarkable that in response to the faith of the men who brought their friend, Jesus forgave his sins and healed his incurable condition!

When someone we know is facing serious physical difficulty or a spiritual crisis, it is our privilege to join together in prayer, bringing our friends to Jesus—the only One who can meet their deepest needs.

—*David McCasland*

Praying for others is a privilege—and a responsibility.

CHRIST-CENTERED FAITH

Read: Colossians 2:1–10

So then, just as you received Christ Jesus as Lord, continue to live your lives in him. —COLOSSIANS 2:6

Some Christians try to live from one dramatic mountaintop experience to another. Their relationship with the Lord is based on their feelings at the moment. They go from Bible conferences to seminars to Bible studies, trying to maintain an emotional high.

Author Creath Davis, referring to his early Christian life, wrote, "I felt that if something spectacular was not transpiring, my faith was weakening. As a result, I missed most of what was going on in the valleys, waiting to get back to the mountain."

What's an effective antidote for a feelings-centered faith? According to the apostle Paul in Colossians 2, being Christ-centered is the answer. Having received Christ Jesus by faith, we are instructed to continue to "live our lives in Him" by faith (v. 6) through both the highs and lows of life. By walking in close fellowship with Him each day, we become "rooted and built up in him, strengthened in the faith" (v. 7). We grow steadily into maturity as we focus on Christ and what He has done for us—not on our feelings.

Mountaintop experiences can be beneficial, but nothing is more profitable than an ongoing, Christ-centered life of faith.

—*Joanie Yoder*

———

True faith needs no feelings to rest upon.

QUIET CONVERSATIONS

Read: Psalm 116:5-9

Praise the LORD, my soul, and forget not all his benefits.
—PSALM 103:2

Do you ever talk to yourself? Sometimes when I'm working on a project—usually under the hood of a car—I find it helpful to think aloud, working through my options on the best way to make the repair. If someone catches me in my "conversation," it can be a little embarrassing—even though talking to ourselves is something most of us do every day.

The psalmists often talked to themselves in the Psalms. The author of Psalm 116 is no exception. In verse 7 he writes, "Return to your rest, my soul, for the LORD has been good to you." Reminding himself of God's kindness and faithfulness in the past is a practical comfort and help to him in the present. We see "conversations" like this frequently in the Psalms. In Psalm 103:1 David tells himself, "Praise the LORD, my soul; all my inmost being, praise his holy name." And in Psalm 62:5 he affirms, "Yes, my soul, find rest in God; my hope comes from him."

It's good to remind ourselves of God's faithfulness and the hope we have in Him. We can follow the example of the psalmist and spend some time naming the many ways God has been good to us. As we do, we'll be encouraged. The same God who has been faithful in the past will continue His love for us in the future.

—*James Banks*

Reminding ourselves about God's goodness can keep us filled with His peace.

COMING ALONGSIDE

Read: Exodus 17:8-16

When Moses' hands grew tired, they took a stone and put it under him and
he sat on it. Aaron and Hur held his hands up—one on one side,
one on the other—so that his hands remained steady till sunset.
—EXODUS 17:12

Her thirty classmates and their parents watched as Mi'Asya nervously walked to the podium to speak at her fifth-grade graduation ceremony. When the principal adjusted the microphone to Mi'Asya's height, Mi'Asya turned her back to the microphone and the audience. The crowd whispered words of encouragement: "Come on, honey, you can do it." But she didn't budge. Then a classmate walked to the front and stood by her side. With the principal on one side of Mi'Asya and her friend on the other, the three read her speech together. What a beautiful example of support!

Moses needed help and support in the middle of a battle with the Amalekites (Exodus 17:10–16). "As long as Moses held up his hands [with the staff of God in his hands], the Israelites were winning, but whenever he lowered his hands, the Amalekites were winning" (v. 11). When Aaron and Hur saw what was happening, they stood beside Moses, "one on one side, one on the other," and supported his arms when he grew tired. With their support, victory came by sunset.

We all need the support of one another. As brothers and sisters in the family of God, we have so many opportunities to encourage one another on our shared journey of faith. And God is right here in our midst giving us His grace to do that.

—*Anne Cetas*

Hope can be ignited
by a spark of encouragement.

SACRIFICIAL FAITH

Read: Acts 6:8-15; 7:59-60

Blessed are those who are persecuted because of righteousness,
for theirs is the kingdom of heaven. —MATTHEW 5:10

It's Sunday afternoon, and I'm sitting in the garden of our home, which is near the church where my husband is the minister. I hear wafts of praise and worship music floating through the air in the Farsi language. Our church in London hosts a vibrant Iranian congregation, and we feel humbled by their passion for Christ as they share some of their stories of persecution and tell of those, such as the senior pastor's brother, who have been martyred for their faith. These faithful believers are following in the footsteps of the first Christian martyr, Stephen.

Stephen, one of the first appointed leaders in the early church, garnered attention in Jerusalem when he performed "great wonders and signs" (Acts 6:8) and was brought before the Jewish authorities to defend his actions. He gave an impassioned defense of the faith before describing the hardheartedness of his accusers. But instead of repenting, they were "furious and gnashed their teeth at him" (7:54). They dragged him from the city and stoned him to death—even as he prayed for their forgiveness.

The stories of Stephen and modern martyrs remind us that the message of Christ can be met with brutality. If we have never faced persecution for our faith, let's pray for the persecuted church around the world. And may we, if and when tested, find grace to be found faithful to the One who suffered so much more for us.

—*Amy Boucher Pye*

May we find grace to walk in the Master's steps.

THE TWELFTH MAN

Read: Hebrews 11:32–12:3

Since we are surrounded by such a great cloud of witnesses, let us throw off everything that hinders and the sin that so easily entangles. And let us run with perseverance the race marked out for us. —HEBREWS 12:1

A large sign at the Texas A&M University football stadium says "HOME OF THE 12TH MAN." While each team is allowed eleven players on the field, the 12th Man is the symbolic name for the thousands of A&M students who remain standing during the entire game to cheer their team on. The tradition traces its roots to 1922 when the coach called a student from the stands to suit up and be ready to replace an injured player. Although he never entered the game, his willing presence on the sideline greatly encouraged the team.

Hebrews 11 describes heroes of the faith who faced great trials and remained loyal to God. Chapter 12 begins, "Therefore, since we are surrounded by such a great cloud of witnesses, let us throw off everything that hinders and the sin that so easily entangles. And let us run with perseverance the race marked out for us" (v. 1).

We are not alone on our journey of faith. The great saints and ordinary people who have been faithful to the Lord encourage us by their example and also by their presence in heaven. They are a spiritual 12th Man standing with us while we are still on the field.

As we fix our eyes on Jesus, "the pioneer and perfecter of faith" (12:2), we are spurred on by all those who followed Him.

—*David McCasland*

Faithful Christians from the past encourage us today.

THE FAITH OF A CHILD

Read: Matthew 21:12-17

The disciples went and did as Jesus had instructed them.
—MATTHEW 21:6

We can be encouraged by the faith of children. They brought encouragement to Jesus as He wrestled the forces of darkness. After He rode on a colt into Jerusalem and entered the temple, the children shouted, "Hosanna to the Son of David!" (Matthew 21:15). When the religious leaders heard them, "they were indignant" (v.15). I can just picture their arrogance as they put the blame on Jesus: "Do You hear what these children are saying?" (v.16).

Of course Jesus had heard them, and He was encouraged. Their young voices ministered to Him during a crucial time. Their cries of praise countered the slanderous attacks of His enemies.

Jesus was in the midst of an intense spiritual battle. Deep in enemy territory, He was opposed by the religious leaders and under attack by satanic foes. The faith and words of these children were a sharp contrast to the insidious voices of the enemies, and their praise supported Him as he made His way to the cross.

When we are burdened by troubles or oppressed by the enemy, it might help us to spend some time with children who know who Jesus is. As we hear of their simple trust in the Lord, our faith can be renewed.

We can learn a lot from the faith of a child.

—*David Egner*

Faith shines brightest in a childlike heart.

HOLD ON

Read: Philippians 3:12–4:1

I have fought the good fight, I have finished the race, I have kept the faith.
—2 TIMOTHY 4:7

Tianmen Mountain in Zhangjiajie, China, is considered one of the most beautiful mountains in the world. To view its towering cliffs in all their glorious splendor, you must take the Tianmen Shan cable car, which covers a distance of 7,455 meters (4.5 miles). It's amazing how this cable car can travel such long distances and scale such steep mountains without any motor on the car itself. Yet it moves safely up these spectacular heights by keeping a strong grip on a cable that is moved by a powerful motor.

In our journey of faith, how can we finish the race well and "press on toward the goal to win the prize for which God has called [us] heavenward in Christ Jesus"? (Philippians 3:14). Like the cable car, we keep a strong grip on Christ, which is what Paul meant when he said, "stand firm in the Lord" (4:1). We have no resources of our own (See John 15:5). We depend fully on Christ to keep us moving forward. He will take us through the greatest challenges and lead us safely home.

Toward the end of his earthly life, the apostle Paul declared, "I have fought the good fight, I have finished the race, I have kept the faith" (2 Timothy 4:7). You can too. Simply keep a strong grip on Christ.

—*Albert Lee*

Keeping the faith means trusting God to faithfully keep you.

CHRISTIANITY'S BEST ARGUMENT

Read: 1 Peter 3:13-17

In your hearts revere Christ as Lord. Always be prepared to give an answer to everyone who asks you to give the reason for the hope that you have.
—1 PETER 3:15

What's the best argument we can give those who ask why we have accepted Jesus as our Savior? How can we most persuasively bear witness to our faith?

"Always be prepared," Peter urged, "to give an answer to everyone who asks you to give the reason for the hope that you have" (1 Peter 3:15). The Greek term for "reason" is *apology*. That doesn't mean a weak-kneed excuse; it means a convincing argument.

Philosopher William Alston of Syracuse University has written very helpful books in defense of the Christian faith. He has something to say that should encourage all of us: "The final test of the Christian scheme comes from trying it out in one's life, testing the promises the scheme tells us God has made, following in the way enjoined on us by the church, and seeing whether it leads to the new life of the Spirit."

Don't think that because you aren't a philosopher or a scholar that you can't be an apologist. You can bear witness to the truth and power of the gospel. Your life can be your own best argument—your best defense of your faith in Jesus Christ—to anyone who asks why you believe.

So put your faith into practice. Let people see the difference Jesus makes.

—*Vernon Grounds*

People will listen to you carefully
if they see you living faithfully.

X

STRANGERS AND FOREIGNERS

Read: Hebrews 11:8-16

For he was looking forward to the city with foundations,
whose architect and builder is God. —HEBREWS 11:10

I parked my bicycle, fingering my map of Cambridge for reassurance. Directions not being my strength, I knew I could easily get lost in this maze of roads bursting with historic buildings.

Life should have felt idyllic, for I had just married my Englishman and moved to the United Kingdom. But I felt adrift. When I kept my mouth closed I blended in, but when I spoke I immediately felt branded as an American tourist. I didn't yet know what my role was, and I quickly realized that blending two stubborn people into one shared life was harder than I had anticipated.

I related to Abraham, who left all that he knew as he obeyed the Lord's call to live as a foreigner and stranger in a new land (Genesis 12:1). He pressed through the cultural challenges while keeping faith in God, and 2,000 years later the writer to the Hebrews named him a hero (11:9). Like the other men and women listed in this chapter, Abraham lived by faith, longing for things promised, hoping and waiting for his heavenly home.

Perhaps you've always lived in the same town. But remember this: As Christ-followers we're all foreigners and strangers on this earth. By faith we press forward, knowing that God will lead and guide us, and by faith we believe He will never leave nor abandon us. By faith we long for home.

—*Amy Boucher Pye*

God calls us to live by faith, believing that He will fulfill His promises.

WHAT FAITH IS AND DOES

Read: Hebrews 11:1-6

Now faith is confidence in what we hope for and assurance about what we do not see. —HEBREWS 11:1

When I was in my mid-teens, I sometimes wondered if my faith was real. I had sincerely placed my trust in Jesus Christ, yet the injustices in society and writings of unbelievers raised doubts in my mind. I didn't dare mention this to anybody. However, I repeatedly committed myself anew to Christ and to His teachings for my life.

Since then, many have told me that they are troubled by the description of faith in Hebrews 11:1. To them it defines faith as absolute intellectual certainty—something they do not always have. But in its context, this verse explains both what faith is and what it does. It affirms the certainty that comes as we continue in our commitment to trust Jesus and His Word. As we do, we become assured of the reality of God and the heaven that awaits us.

To test the validity of this statement, consider the steadfast faith of elderly believers who have continued trusting Jesus through great trials, sorrow, and pain. They will tell you that Jesus has become so real and precious to them that they are absolutely sure of Him and the truthfulness of His promises.

Don't let times of doubt discourage you. Keep trusting and obeying the Lord Jesus and His Word. As you do, your confidence will grow.

—*Herb Vander Lugt*

Feed your faith, and your doubts will starve.

OUR SOURCE OF HELP

Read: Psalm 121

My help comes from the LORD, the Maker of heaven and earth.
—PSALM 121:2

Twenty-year-old Lygon Stevens, an experienced mountaineer, had reached the summits of Mount Denali, Mount Rainier, four Andean peaks in Ecuador, and thirty-nine of Colorado's highest mountains. "I climb because I love the mountains," she said, "and I meet God there." In January 2008, Lygon died in an avalanche while climbing Little Bear Peak in southern Colorado with her brother Nicklis, who survived.

When her parents discovered her journals, they were deeply moved by the intimacy of her walk with Christ. "Always a shining light for Him," her mother said, "Lygon experienced a depth and honesty in her relationship with the Lord, which even seasoned veterans of faith long to have."

In Lygon's final journal entry, written from her tent three days before the avalanche, she said: "God is good, and He has a plan for our lives that is greater and more blessed than the lives we pick out for ourselves, and I am so thankful about that. Thank you, Lord, for bringing me this far and to this place. I leave the rest—my future—in those same hands and say thank you."

Lygon echoed these words from the psalmist: "My help comes from the LORD, the maker of heaven and earth" (Psalm 121:2).

—*David McCasland*

We can trust our all-knowing God for the unknown future.

STANDING ON THE EDGE

Read: Joshua 3:9-17

When the people broke camp to cross the Jordan, the priests carrying the ark of the covenant went ahead of them. —JOSHUA 3:14

My little girl stood apprehensively at the pool's edge. As a nonswimmer, she was just learning to become comfortable in the water. Her instructor waited in the pool with outstretched arms. As my daughter hesitated, I saw the questions in her eyes: Will you catch me? What will happen if my head goes under?

The Israelites may have wondered what would happen when they crossed the Jordan River. Could they trust God to make dry ground appear in the riverbed? Was God guiding their new leader, Joshua, as He had led Moses? Would God help His people defeat the threatening Canaanites who lived just across the river?

To learn the answers to these questions, the Israelites had to engage in a test of faith—they had to act. So "when the people broke camp to cross the Jordan, the priests carrying the ark of the covenant went ahead of them" (Joshua 3:14). Exercising their faith allowed them to see that God was with them. He was still directing Joshua, and He would help them settle in Canaan (vv. 7, 10, 17).

If you are facing a test of faith, you too can move forward based on God's character and His unfailing promises. Relying on Him will help you move from where you are to where He wants you to be.

—*Jennifer Benson Schuldt*

Fear fades when we trust our Father.

PANNING FOR GOLD

Read: Luke 18:18-30

These have come so that the proven genuineness of your faith—of greater worth than gold, which perishes even though refined by fire—may result in praise, glory and honor when Jesus Christ is revealed. —1 PETER 1:7

While on vacation in Alaska, we visited the El Dorado Gold Mine near Fairbanks. After a tour and demonstrations of mining techniques during Gold Rush days, we got to do a little panning for gold. Each person was given a pan and a bag of dirt and stones. After pouring the contents into the pan, we added water from a trough and swirled it around to stir up the silt and allow the gold, which is heavy, to sink to the bottom. Even though we had watched experts, we made little progress. The reason? Concerned about discarding something of value, we were unwilling to throw away worthless stones.

This reminded me of how possessions sometimes keep us from finding what is truly valuable. Jesus had an encounter with a rich man for whom this was true. His earthly wealth was more important to him than spiritual treasure (Luke 18:18–30). Jesus said, "How hard it is for the rich to enter the kingdom of God!" (v. 24).

Although money is not evil, it can prevent us from inheriting true riches if accumulating it is the goal of our lives. To hoard wealth is foolish, for it is genuine faith, not gold, that will sustain us through trials and result in praise, honor, and glory to God (1 Peter 1:7).

—*Julie Ackerman Link*

Keep your eyes on Jesus so you don't
allow earthly riches to blind you
to spiritual riches.

MAILBOX FAITH

Read: Hebrews 11:1-6

Now faith is confidence in what we hope for and assurance about what we do not see. —HEBREWS 11:1

Whenever I mail a letter, it's an exercise of trust. Let me explain what I mean. When I write to a distant friend, it's impossible to deliver the letter myself. I need the help of the postal service. But for them to do their part, I have to drop my letter in the mailbox first. I can't hang on to it. I have to place it in the mail slot and let go. Then I must trust the postal service to take over until my letter is delivered to my friend's home. Although I can't see what happens to it, my faith in the postal service assures me that my letter is as good as there!

Likewise, whenever we're faced with a problem, our faith is challenged. Knowing that it's impossible to resolve the difficulty ourselves, we recognize our need of God's help. First, though, we must go to Him in prayer. Until that moment, we're still holding on to our problem. We know the situation won't get resolved until we let go and commit it into God's hands. Once we let go, we then must trust God to take over until the problem is resolved in His way. Although we can't see what He's doing, our faith is "the evidence of things not seen" (Hebrews 11:1 NKJV), the assurance that His work is as good as done!

Have you exercised trust in Him today?

—*Joanie Yoder*

Trusting God turns problems into opportunities.

THE VOICE OF FAITH

Read: Habakkuk 3:16–19

Though the fig tree does not bud and there are no grapes on the vines, though the olive crop fails and the fields produce no food, though there are no sheep in the pen and no cattle in the stalls, yet I will rejoice in the LORD, I will be joyful in God my Savior. —HABAKKUK 3:17–18

The news was numbing. The tears came so quickly that she couldn't fight them. Her mind raced with questions, and fear threatened to overwhelm her. Life had been going along so well, when it was abruptly interrupted and forever changed without warning.

Tragedy can come in many forms—the loss of a loved one, an illness, the loss of wealth or our livelihood. And it can happen to anyone at any time.

Although the prophet Habakkuk knew that tragedy was coming, it still struck fear in his heart. As he waited for the day when Babylon would invade the kingdom of Judah, his heart pounded, his lips quivered, and his legs trembled (Habakkuk 3:16).

Fear is a legitimate emotion in the face of tragedy, but it doesn't have to immobilize us. When we don't understand the trials we are going through, we can recount how God has worked in history (vv. 3–15). That's what Habakkuk did. It didn't dispel his fear, but it gave him the courage to move on by choosing to praise the Lord (v. 18).

Our God who has proven himself faithful throughout the years is always with us. Because His character doesn't change, in our fear we can say with a confident voice of faith, "The Sovereign LORD is my strength!" (v. 19).

—Poh Fang Chia

We can learn the lesson of trust in the school of trial.

THE GROWTH CHART

Read 2 Peter 3:10-18

But grow in the grace and knowledge of our Lord and Savior Jesus Christ. To him be glory both now and forever! Amen. —2 PETER 3:18

If my family ever moves from the house where we live now, I want to unhinge the pantry door and take it with me! That door is special because it shows how my children have grown over the years. Every few months, my husband and I place our children against the door and pencil a mark just above their heads. According to our growth chart, my daughter shot up four inches in just one year!

While my children grow physically as a natural part of life, there's another kind of growth that happens with some effort—our spiritual growth in Christlikeness. Peter encouraged believers to "grow in the grace and knowledge" of Jesus (2 Peter 3:18). He said that maturing in our faith prepares us for Christ's return. The apostle wanted Jesus to come back and find believers living in peace and righteousness (v. 14). Peter viewed spiritual growth as a defense against teaching that incorrectly interprets God's Word and leads people astray (vv. 16–17).

Even when we feel discouraged and disconnected from God, we can remember that He will help us advance in our faith by making us more like His Son. His Word assures us that "he who began a good work in [us] will carry it on to completion until the day of Christ Jesus" (Philippians 1:6).

—*Jennifer Benson Schuldt*

Spiritual growth requires the solid food of God's Word.

DOUBTS AND FAITH

Read: John 20:24-31

Thomas said to him, "My Lord and my God!" —JOHN 20:28

Can a believer in Jesus who has occasional doubts about matters of faith ever be effective in serving the Lord? Some people think that mature and growing Christians never question their beliefs. But just as we have experiences that can build our faith, we can also have experiences that cause us to temporarily doubt.

The disciple Thomas had initial doubts about reports of Jesus's resurrection. He said, "Unless I see the nail marks in his hands, . . . I will not believe" (John 20:25). Christ did not rebuke Thomas but showed him the evidence he asked for. Amazed at seeing the risen Savior, Thomas exclaimed: "My Lord and my God!" (20:28). After this incident, the New Testament says very little about what happened to Thomas.

A number of early church traditions, however, claim that Thomas went to India as a missionary. It is said that while there he preached the gospel, worked miracles, and planted churches. Some of these churches in India still have active congregations that trace their founding back to Thomas.

A time of doubt doesn't have to become a life pattern. Allow God to lead you into a deeper understanding of His reality. Renew your faith. You can still accomplish great things for Him.

—Dennis Fisher

Learn to doubt your doubts and believe your beliefs.

EYEWITNESS

Read: 1 John 1:1-7

Through [Jesus] all things were made; without him
nothing was made that has been made. —JOHN 1:3

"You don't want to interview me for your television program,"
the man told me. "You need someone who is young and pho-
togenic, and I'm neither." I replied that we indeed wanted him
because he had known C. S. Lewis, the noted author and the
subject of the documentary we were producing. "Sir," I said,
"when it comes to telling the story of a person's life, there is no
substitute for an eyewitness."

As Christians, we often refer to sharing our faith in Christ
as "witnessing" or "giving our testimony." It's an accurate
concept taken directly from the Bible. John, a companion and
disciple of Jesus, wrote this: "We have seen, and bear witness,
and declare to you that eternal life which was with the Father
and was manifested to us—that which we have seen and heard
we declare to you" (1 John 1:2–3 NKJV).

If you know Jesus as your Savior and have experienced
His love, grace, and forgiveness, you can tell someone else
about Him. Youth, beauty, and theological training are not
required. Reality and enthusiasm are more valuable than a
training course in how to share your faith.

When it comes to telling someone the wonderful story of
how Jesus Christ can transform a person's life, there is no substitute for a firsthand witness like you.

—*David McCasland*

Jesus doesn't need lawyers,
He needs witnesses.

SECONDHAND FAITH

Read Judges 2:6–12

*After that whole generation had been gathered to their ancestors,
another generation grew up who knew neither the LORD nor
what he had done for Israel.* —JUDGES 2:10

When I was growing up in Singapore, some of my school friends were kicked out of their homes by their non-Christian parents for daring to believe in Jesus Christ. They suffered for their beliefs and emerged with stronger convictions. By contrast, I was born and raised in a Christian family. Though I didn't suffer persecution, I too had to make faith my own.

The Israelites who first entered the Promised Land with Joshua saw the mighty acts of God and believed (Judges 2:7). But sadly, the very next generation "knew neither the LORD nor what he had done for Israel" (v. 10). So it was not long before they turned aside to worship other gods (v. 12). They didn't make their parents' faith their own.

No generation can live off the faith of the previous generation. Every generation needs a firsthand faith. When faced with trouble of any kind, the faith that is not personalized is likely to drift and falter.

Those who are second, third, or even fourth generation Christians have a wonderful legacy, to be sure. However, there's no secondhand faith! Find out what God says in His Word and personalize it so that yours is a fresh, firsthand faith (Joshua 1:8).

—*C. P. Hia*

If your faith is not personalized, it's not faith.

EXPECT GREAT THINGS

Read: Hebrews 11:32-40

Who through faith conquered kingdoms, administered justice, and gained what was promised; who shut the mouths of lions, quenched the fury of the flames, and escaped the edge of the sword; whose weakness was turned to strength; and who became powerful in battle and routed foreign armies.
—HEBREWS 11:33–34

William Carey was an ordinary man with an extraordinary faith. Born into a working-class family in eighteenth-century England (1761–1834), Carey made his living as a shoemaker. While crafting shoes, Carey read theology and journals of explorers. God used His Word and the stories of the discovery of new people groups to burden him for global evangelism. He went to India as a missionary, and not only did he do the work of an evangelist but he also learned Indian dialects into which he translated the Word of God. Carey's passion for missions is expressed by his words: "Expect great things from God; attempt great things for God." Carey lived out this maxim, and thousands have been inspired to do missionary service by his example.

The Bible tells of many whose faith in God produced amazing results. Hebrews tells of those "who through faith conquered kingdoms, administered justice, and gained what was promised; who shut the mouths of lions, quenched the fury of the flames, and escaped the edge of the sword; whose weakness was turned to strength" (11:33–34).

The list of heroes of the faith has grown through the ages, and we can be a part of that list. Because of God's power and faithfulness, we can attempt great things for God and expect great things from God.

—*Dennis Fisher*

When God is your partner, you can make your plans large!

WALKING OUR FAITH

Read: Romans 2:17-24

You see that his faith and his actions were working together, and his faith was made complete by what he did. —JAMES 2:22

Often we Christians are urged to "walk the talk," not just "talk the talk." The same advice may be expressed in these words: "Don't let your behavior contradict your professed belief." At other times we are admonished to be sure that life and lip agree. If our conduct doesn't harmonize with our confession of faith, however, that discrepancy nullifies the testimony of the gospel we proclaim.

As far as we can know, Mahatma Gandhi never became a Christian, but he made a statement that we who follow Jesus would do well to ponder. When asked to put his message into one short sentence, he replied, "My life is my message."

Certainly we should explain the gospel message as clearly as possible. Yet the clearest explanation isn't going to win hearts for our Lord unless His love is embodied in our lives. To quote the apostle Paul in 1 Corinthians 11:1, "Imitate me, just as I also imitate Christ" (NKJV). Holding himself up as a pattern, he also said, "Whatever you have learned or received or heard from me, or seen in me—put it into practice. And the God of peace will be with you" (Philippians 4:9).

Like Paul, we can live out our saving faith before the watching world.

—*Vernon Grounds*

The world is watching us—do they see Jesus?

GOD'S PLAN, NOT OURS

Read: 1 Samuel 4:1-21

*I will say of the LORD, "He is my refuge and my fortress,
my God, in whom I trust."* —PSALM 91:2

Everybody was wrong about the ark of the covenant (an item in the tabernacle that represented the throne of God). After losing a battle to the Philistines, Israel sent messengers to Shiloh to ask that the ark be hauled to Ebenezer, the site of their army camp.

When the ark arrived, the Israelites celebrated so loudly the enemy heard them all the way over in Aphek. The ark's arrival caused the Philistines to fear and the Israelites to have courage.

They were both wrong. First, the Israelites took the ark into battle and were again clobbered by the Philistines, who captured the ark. Then, while the ark was in their possession, the Philistines got sick and their false gods were destroyed.

We can understand the Philistines' error—they were idol-worshipers. But the Israelites should have known better. They failed to consult God about using the ark. While they knew that the ark was earlier carried in battle (Joshua 6), they didn't consider that God's plan, not the ark's involvement, allowed Israel to defeat Jericho.

No matter our resources, we will fail unless we use them according to God's plan. Let's study the Word, pray for God's direction, and trust His leading (Psalm 91:2) before we step out in any venture of faith.

—*Dave Branon*

We see in part; God sees the whole.

GOD-CENTERED FAITH

Read: Mark 11:12–24

"Have faith in God," Jesus answered. —MARK 11:22

During difficult times we often lament, "If only I had more faith!" Yet we demonstrate in everyday life that the most important issue is not the amount of our faith but the object of our faith. For instance, whenever we sit down in a chair, we trust that it will support us. Our faith is in the chair, not in how much faith we possess.

In Mark 11:12–24, Jesus taught His disciples the importance of having the right object of faith. It began when they overheard Jesus curse a fig tree (v. 14). The next morning, Peter exclaimed, "Look! The fig tree you cursed has withered" (v. 21). Jesus replied, "Have faith in God" (v. 22). Having declared to His followers that God was the object of faith, Jesus assured them that they too could pray for and receive amazing results through God-centered faith. And so may we.

Often, however, we praise those who have great faith in God. Ian Thomas once preached: "When we congratulate people for having faith in our Creator, we're really saying that God is so decrepit they're to be congratulated for believing in Him." He continued, "To become less conscious of faith, we must become more acquainted with the object of faith."

Get to know God better. Then trusting Him will become as natural as trusting the chair you're sitting on!

—*Joanie Yoder*

Our faith may not be great
but our God is.

Ж

VALID ENTRY

Read: John 14:1-10

Jesus answered, "I am the way and the truth and the life. No one comes to the Father except through me." —JOHN 14:6

On a teaching trip outside the US, my wife and I were denied entry into our country of destination because of visa problems. Although we were under the assumption our visas had been correctly issued by the country we planned to visit, they were deemed invalid. Despite the efforts of several government officials, nothing could be done. We weren't allowed in. We were placed on the next flight back to the States. No amount of intervention could change the fact that we did not have the proper validation for entrance.

That experience with my visa was inconvenient, but it can't begin to compare with the ultimate entry rejection. I'm speaking of those who will stand before God without valid entry into heaven. What if they were to present the record of their religious efforts and good deeds? That would not be enough. What if they were to call character references? That wouldn't work. Only one thing can give anyone entry into heaven. Jesus said, "I am the way and the truth and the life. No one comes to the Father except through me" (John 14:6).

Christ alone, through His death and resurrection, paid the price for our sins. And only He can give us valid entry into the presence of the Father. Have you put your faith in Jesus? Make sure you have a valid entry into heaven.

—*Bill Crowder*

Only through Christ can we enter the Father's presence.

A CRUTCH?

Read: 2 Corinthians 4:8–15

We are hard pressed on every side, but not crushed; perplexed,
but not in despair. —2 CORINTHIANS 4:8

Have you ever heard skeptics say that the Christian faith is nothing more than a crutch—that the only reason people claim to trust Jesus is that they are weaklings who have to make up "religion" to get by?

Apparently those skeptics haven't heard about the doctor in one Far Eastern country who spent two-and-a-half years in jail being "reeducated" because he professed faith in Christ. Then, after his release, he was arrested again—this time for his efforts at his church.

And perhaps those skeptics haven't heard about Paul. After trusting Christ, he was arrested, flogged, mocked, and ship-wrecked (2 Corinthians 11:16–29).

These believers were not looking for a crutch. No, they had something deep and essential in their hearts. They had a personal relationship with God—a relationship born of faith in the work of Jesus on the cross. As a result, they became children of the King—eager to sacrifice everything for the privilege of proclaiming Him. They were not limping along looking for something to hold them up.

A crutch? Hardly. Faith in Christ is not about safety and caution. It's about believing Jesus and trusting Him no matter what. It's about taking up a daily cross (Luke 9:23) and living for the Savior.

—*Dave Branon*

———

Because Jesus bore the cross for us, we willingly take it up for Him.

GOD'S WHEELCHAIR

Read: Psalm 46

"As I looked, thrones were set in place, and the Ancient of Days took his seat. His clothing was as white as snow; the hair of his head was white like wool. His throne was flaming with fire, and its wheels were all ablaze." —DANIEL 7:9

Jean Driscoll is a remarkable athlete. She has won the Boston Marathon eight times. She has also participated in four Paralympic Games and won five gold medals. Born with spina bifida, Jean competes in a wheelchair.

One of Driscoll's favorite Bible verses is Daniel 7:9, "The Ancient of Days took his seat . . . . His throne was flaming with fire, its wheels were all ablaze." Seeing a connection between Daniel's vision of God and her own situation, she is able to pass along words of encouragement to others. "Anytime I've had an opportunity to talk with people who use wheelchairs and feel bad about being in a chair," Jean says, "I tell them, 'Not only are you made in the image of God, but your wheelchair is made in the image of His throne!'"

Daniel's vision, of course, doesn't portray God as being impaired in motion. In fact, some see God's "wheelchair" as a symbol of a just God sovereignly moving within human affairs. Other passages speak of God's providence providing help to those who believe (Proverbs 3:25–26; Matthew 20:29–34; Ephesians 1:11).

Jean Driscoll's faith in God has helped her triumph over personal challenges. We too can be confident that the high and holy One is near and ready to help us if only we ask (Psalm 46).

—*Dennis Fisher*

With God behind you and His arms beneath you, you can face whatever lies ahead of you. —Ward

UNANSWERED PRAYER

Read: Luke 7:1-10

When Jesus heard this, he was amazed at him, and turning to the crowd following him, he said, "I tell you, I have not found such great faith even in Israel." —LUKE 7:9

An explanation we often hear for "unanswered" prayers is that we don't have enough faith. But Jesus said in Luke 17:6 that if we have faith the size of a mustard seed, we can command a mulberry tree to be uprooted and planted in the sea and it will obey us. In other words, the effectiveness of our prayers depends not on how much faith we have but on whether we even have faith.

Luke tells of a Roman centurion with "great faith" (7:9). His faith was expressed first as an appeal to Jesus to heal his dying servant. Then it was expressed as an acknowledgment that Jesus could heal his servant anytime, anywhere. The centurion did not ask Jesus to do things his way.

Faith has been described as "trusting God's heart and trusting God's power." Some prayers that seem to go unanswered are simply instances in which God has lovingly overruled our wishes. He knows that what we have asked for is not best. Or it may be that our timing is not His timing, or He has some far greater purpose in mind. Let us remember, even Jesus prayed to His heavenly Father, "Not my will, but yours be done" (Luke 22:42).

Do we have the centurion's great faith—a faith that trusts God to do His work in His way?

—C. P. Hia

God's answers are wiser than our prayers.

FAITH THAT WORKS

Read: James 2:14-26

As the body without the spirit is dead, so faith without deeds is dead.
—JAMES 2:26

Mary is a senior citizen with many health problems. She is also a widow with a home to keep up. No use expecting Mary to do much in the church or community anymore, right? Wrong! In spite of her limitations, her faith continues to work.

Although Mary and her late husband had no children, they had a ministry to other people's children. Now alone, she coordinates a new ministry in her church for women who might be considering abortion.

Mary writes, "If we are preaching against abortion, we should offer pregnant women our help. Within two days I've had four volunteers to help me. Now we must meet to set up a plan of action."

A plan of action—how typical of a working faith! How different from people who see a desperate need and moan, "Why doesn't somebody do something?" but are unwilling to be that somebody!

In James 2 we read that Abraham obediently offered his son Isaac on the altar. This act is cited as a work that proved the reality of his faith (vv. 21–23).

Mary, like Abraham, has a faith that works. Our needy world could use many more like them. How can you put your faith into action today?

—*Joanie Yoder*

Faith never stands around
with its hands in its pockets.

NO HOPE BUT GOD

Read: Romans 5:1-5

But if we hope for what we do not yet have, we wait for it patiently.
—ROMANS 8:25

In his book *Through the Valley of the Kwai*, Scottish officer Ernest Gordon wrote of his years as a prisoner of war during World War II. The 6' 2" man suffered from malaria, diphtheria, typhoid, beriberi, dysentery, and jungle ulcers, and the hard labor and scarcity of food quickly plunged his weight to less than 100 pounds.

The squalor of the prison hospital prompted a desperate Ernest to request to be moved to a cleaner place—the morgue. Lying in the dirt of the death house, he waited to die. But every day, a fellow prisoner came to wash his wounds and to encourage him to eat part of his own rations. As the quiet and unassuming Dusty Miller nursed Ernest back to health, he talked with the agnostic Scotsman of his own strong faith in God and showed him that—even in the midst of suffering—there is hope.

The hope we read about in Scripture is not a vague, wishy-washy optimism. Instead, biblical hope is a strong and confident expectation that what God has promised in His Word He will accomplish. Tribulation is often the catalyst that produces perseverance, character, and finally, hope (Romans 5:3–4).

Seventy years ago, in a brutal POW camp, Ernest Gordon learned this truth himself and said, "Faith thrives when there is no hope but God" (see Romans 8:24–25).

—*Cindy Hess Kasper*

Christ, the Rock, is our sure hope.

OUR DAILY BREAD WRITERS

JAMES BANKS

Pastor of Peace Church in Durham, North Carolina, Dr. James Banks has written several books for Discovery House, including *Praying Together* and *Prayers for Prodigals.*

DAVE BRANON

An editor with Discovery House, Dave has been involved with *Our Daily Bread* since the 1980s. He has written several books, including *Beyond the Valley* and *Stand Firm,* both DH publications.

ANNE CETAS

After becoming a Christian in her late teens, Anne was introduced to *Our Daily Bread* right away and began reading it. Now she reads it for a living as the managing editor of *Our Daily Bread.*

POH FANG CHIA

Like Anne Cetas, Poh Fang trusted Jesus Christ as Savior as a teenager. She is an editor and a part of the Chinese editorial review committee serving in the Our Daily Bread Ministries Singapore office.

BILL CROWDER

A former pastor who is now an associate teacher for Our Daily Bread Ministries, Bill travels extensively as a Bible conference teacher, sharing God's truths with fellow believers in Malaysia and Singapore and other places where ODB Ministries has international offices. His Discovery House books include *Windows on Easter* and *Let's Talk*.

DENNIS DEHAAN

When Henry Bosch retired, Dennis became the second managing editor of *Our Daily Bread*. A former pastor, he loved preaching and teaching the Word of God. Dennis went to be with the Lord in 2014.

MART DEHAAN

The former president of Our Daily Bread Ministries, Mart followed in the footsteps of his grandfather M. R. and his dad Richard in that capacity. Mart, who has long been associated with *Day of Discovery* as host of the program from Israel, is now senior content advisor for Our Daily Bread Ministries.

RICHARD DEHAAN

Son of the founder of Our Daily Bread Ministries, Dr. M. R. DeHaan, Richard was responsible for the ministry's entrance into television. Under his leadership, *Day of Discovery* television made its debut in 1968. Richard entered heaven's glories in 2002.

DAVID EGNER

A retired Our Daily Bread Ministries editor and longtime *Our Daily Bread* writer, David was also a college professor during his working career. In fact, he was a writing instructor for both Anne Cetas and Julie Ackerman Link at Cornerstone University.

DENNIS FISHER

As a senior research editor at Our Daily Bread Ministries, Dennis uses his theological training to guarantee biblical accuracy. He is also an expert in C. S. Lewis studies.

VERNON GROUNDS

A longtime college president (Denver Seminary) and board member for Our Daily Bread Ministries, Vernon's life story was told in the Discovery House book *Transformed by Love*. Dr. Grounds died in 2010 at the age of 96.

TIM GUSTAFSON

Tim writes for *Our Daily Bread* and *Our Daily Journey* and serves as an editor for Discovery Series. As the son of missionaries to Ghana, Tim has an unusual perspective on life in the West. He and his wife, Leisa, are the parents of one daughter and seven sons.

C. P. HIA

Serving in the Our Daily Bread Ministries Singapore office, C. P. loves to teach the Bible. He sometimes assists with the Discovery Series Bible Studies from Our Daily Bread Ministries.

CINDY HESS KASPER

An editor for the Our Daily Bread Ministries publication *Our Daily Journey*, Cindy began writing for *Our Daily Bread* in 2006. She and her husband, Tom, have three children and seven grandchildren.

RANDY KILGORE

Randy spent most of his twenty-plus years in business as a senior human resource manager before returning to seminary. Since finishing his Masters in Divinity in 2000, he has served as a writer and workplace chaplain. A collection of his devotionals appears in the Discovery House book, *Made to Matter: Devotions for Working Christians*. Randy and his wife, Cheryl, and their two children live in Massachusetts.

ALBERT LEE

For several years, Albert Lee was director of international ministries for Our Daily Bread Ministries while writing for *Our Daily Bread*.

JULIE ACKERMAN LINK

A book editor by profession, Julie began writing for *Our Daily Bread* in 2000. Her books *Above All, Love* and *A Heart for God* are available through Discovery House. Julie lost her long battle with cancer in April 2015.

DAVID MCCASLAND

Living in Colorado, David enjoys the beauty of God's grandeur as displayed in the Rocky Mountains. An accomplished biographer, David has written several books, including the award-winning *Oswald Chambers: Abandoned to God*, and *Eric Liddell: Pure Gold*.

KEILA OCHOA

From her home in Mexico, Keila assists with Media Associates International, a group that trains writers around the world to write about faith. She and her husband have two young children.

AMY BOUCHER PYE

Amy is a writer, editor, and speaker. The author of *Finding Myself in Britain: Our Search for Faith, Home, and True Identity*, she runs the Woman Alive book club in the UK and enjoys life with her family in their English vicarage.

DAVID ROPER

David Roper lives in Idaho, where he takes advantage of the natural beauty of his state. He has been writing for *Our Daily Bread* since 2000, and he has published several successful books with Discovery House, including *Out of the Ordinary* and *Teach Us To Number Our Days*.

JENNIFER BENSON SCHULDT

Chicagoan Jennifer Schuldt writes from the perspective of a mom of a growing family. She has written for *Our Daily Bread* since 2010, and she also pens articles for another Our Daily Bread Ministries publication: *Our Daily Journey*.

HERB VANDER LUGT

For many years, Herb was senior research editor at Our Daily Bread Ministries, responsible for checking the biblical accuracy of the booklets published by ODB Ministries. A World War II veteran, Herb spent several years as a pastor before his ODB tenure began. Herb went to be with his Lord and Savior in 2006.

PAUL VAN GORDER

A writer for *Our Daily Bread* in the 1980s and 1990s, Paul was a noted pastor and Bible teacher—both in the Atlanta area where he lived and through the *Day of Discovery* TV program. Paul's earthly journey ended in 2009.

JOANIE YODER

For ten years, until her death in 2004, Joanie wrote for *Our Daily Bread*. In addition, she published the book *God Alone* with Discovery House.

SCRIPTURE INDEX
OF KEY VERSES

NOTE TO THE READER

The publisher invites you to share your response to the message of this book by writing Discovery House, P.O. Box 3566, Grand Rapids, MI 49501, USA. For information about other Discovery House books, music, or DVDs, contact us at the same address or call 1-800-653-8333. Find us online at dhp.org or send e-mail to books@dhp.org.